Book 2

Thoughts On:

Post-Truth Politics
&
Magical Thinking

by

Ramsey Dukes

The Mouse That Spins
2019

Published by The Mouse that Spins
2019

Copyright © Lionel Snell
ISBN 0-903411-50-3

Preface

In recent years I have posted a number of short videos on the Ramsey Dukes YouTube channel on several themes around magic and the occult. These videos have been well received, and some people suggested that they might like the content to be available in print or e-book format.

This book is based on transcripts of videos that I collected under the playlist *Post truth politics, Brexit and trumped up frenzy* – a bit different from my core interests, but I do explain and justify their relevance to my ideas. I have edited them to remove the "ums" and "you knows" of unscripted rambling, and also tidied some of the wording for greater clarity. When I had the energy, I also updated or amplified some of the arguments. So a lot of the material is not new, but the presentation in this form and in this sequence might be useful.

This is the second in a series of such booklets based on linked themes from my YouTube channel. The first was *Thoughts on Abramelin*.

Ramsey Dukes

The Ramsey Dukes YouTube Channel:
https://www.youtube.com/channel/UC8-NwOu0WV5Qd_U4zOP33sw

Contents

Introduction

I was writing a book about the rise in magical thinking when I started my YouTube videos. Unlike other commentators, who deplored magical thinking, I argued that the trend had its positive aspects.

Whereas traditional cultures paid homage to The Good, The Beautiful and The True, I suggested that the Protestant revolution had demoted The Beautiful as "worldly indulgence", replacing the music of scripture read aloud in Latin with a vernacular version to be taken as literal truth. The resulting scientific revolution had demoted The Good to leave only The True, a single dimension of human experience spanning truth and illusion. Then digitization reduced that dimension to a simple binary state: True or False. Whether something exists or not is now its fundamental measure of worth.

Aleister Crowley argued that it is immaterial whether magical ideas exist or not: "By doing certain things certain results will follow; students are most earnestly warned against attributing objective reality or philosophic validity to any of them." Thus he welcomed a fourth principle, The Effective, which could co-exist happily with The Beautiful and The Good and be recognised as the guiding principle of magical thinking.

The problem with anything that reduces experience to a binary state is that it sees in dissent naught but enmity. So the non-truth aspects of magical thinking requires that it be cast into the same pit as a host of post and anti-truth demons.

This is bollocks. Magical thinking puts Truth back where it belongs: on the same level as Beauty, Goodness and Effectiveness.

Post truth politics and magical thinking

I was preparing a book – where I take a positive stance about the value of magical thinking and its potential to liberate us from the tyranny of unalloyed truth – when I came across an article in The Economist *raising issues that I needed to consider*

September the 10th Economist had a headline article *The art of the lie* subtitled *Post truth politics in the age of social media*. That article drew critical attention to the spread of what they called "post truth politics" – in other words a world where it doesn't matter whether something is true as long as what you say feels right, or is the most effective statement to win mass approval. The same value judgement is associated with magical thinking, where truth is of secondary importance, not primary importance.

This was interesting to me, because in the book I'm currently publishing, called *My Years of Magical Thinking*[1], I argue that something similar happened 2,000 years ago. Following some five centuries of the Greek classical era, with its emphasis on rationalism and the quest for truth, there came the Roman era, marked by a rise in magical thinking – and I suggested that something very similar is happening now. Today's magical thinking is also associated with a shift from truth being the prime consideration towards a greater emphasis on what feels right or is most useful or effective.

---

[1] Published in 2017, Paperback ISBN-13: 978-0904311242, also Hardback and Kindle editions.

I was brought up in the 1950s, a decade of extreme rationalism. So I was trained to equate truth with righteousness and was never very good at the sort of social niceties that downgrade the importance of truth. Customs that require one to say "you're looking so much better" when someone is dying, or "how lovely, that really suits you" when someone has a ridiculous haircut. Such statements are justifiable as good magic, because they work.

In my book I associated this evolution with the shift from Platonic idealism towards Aristotelian pragmatism. It was a shift from the Platonic notion that our subjective world is a world of shadows that we mistake for reality, whereas if we were to turn around and see the cave entrance, the light streaming in and the real objects casting those shadows, then we would know the truth – something of greater value because it is objective and eternal compared with those subjective shadows. That was a very powerful notion and it held sway for centuries. But his pupil, Aristotle, presented an alternative, data-driven argument: if we have evolved senses that experience this subjective world, then surely human knowledge ought to begin by exploring the data provided by that subjective experience, before going on to seek objective truths reflected in that data.

If we were fish in a pond, it would be all very well to speculate about a greater world of air up above our experience, but surely we should begin by mastering the medium we're in – to get to know the actual world we live in rather than speculating about whatever higher truth lies out there. This is not to say that metaphysical speculation is not interesting – it might actually be very important – but let us first explore, understand and master the data presented by our given senses.

Consider someone madly in love with their neighbor's wife: an amazing experience, the torments and the joys. Then one Platonist reveals the truth that actually this is

Satan tempting him from the path of righteousness: another Platonist insists that it is just his genes wanting to propagate themselves; and a third reveals the truth that it is his hormones causing this experience – each offering a "true explanation" of the shadow world of mad love. Are these true explanations really so much more valuable than the experience of falling in love?

In an artistic culture the experience might inspire a poem, a picture, or musical composition. In a magical culture, a New Ager might use the experience to discover their inner feminine, or a traditional magician or pagan might seek to form a relationship with the goddess. There is so much that one could do with that wonderful subjective experience – beyond simply saying: "it's a hormone imbalance that can be cured with suitable medication".

I also used the metaphor of a great movie. One can enjoy it as an experience: it could be life-changing, or one could write a thesis on the themes of this great movie. Or else a sceptic could say that it is just actors and special effects – nothing real. Or a scientist might look at the DVD or Blue Ray disc through a microscope and announce that it is simply a long string of digital information: that is all you have really experienced. Such people seem to think that their revelation of such objective truth is of greater value than the richness of subjective experience, to the extent that it degrades the latter as "mere illusion."

Similarly, I argue that a good tarot, clairvoyant or astrology reading can be a life changing experience if you know how to use it and how to really work with it. This can often yield greater value than the "truth" that it might just be your brain seeing patterns that are not really there, or that you might be fooled by a cold reader. I am not saying such revelations are of no interest, but that they might offer less value than an acceptance of the reading experience.

So this is how I was experiencing the shift from truth as the main arbiter, towards a recognition of what feels right, or is more effective or useful in your immediate situation.

It was, however, clear from The Economist article that some people find this trend very disturbing. And, when they present examples like Brexit, Trump and Putin, then the idea of playing with truth becomes a lot less attractive. So is this the sort of magical thinking that I am advocating?

No, I too find these political influences quite disturbing. I see a parallel with some YouTube videos of Richard Dawkins interviewing Derren Brown for a series called *The Enemies of Truth*. In it Dawkins emphasises the negative aspects of cold reading: how some crooks cheat gullible people by pretending that they can speak to dead relatives, or that they have psychic knowledge. Dawkins is campaigning vigorously against such people and presenting it as an attack on psychism itself – when it should rather be an attack on confidence tricksters.

You see, I get enormous amount of spam mail trying to lure me into spending money. Despite my obvious interest in things magical, these persuaders are not pretending to be psychic or to predict my future, instead they try to fool me with bogus scientific or statistical claims such as algorithms to make me a fortune on spread betting, or miracle remedies backed by research with reference to "scientific" journals. On such evidence, one might argue against science by emphasising its exploitation to kill people and destroy the environment. Following Richard Dawkins' example, one might campaign to describe scientists as "the enemies of the people" and argue that science should be made illegal. Instead I argue that we need better understanding of science, better scientific education.

If we recognise a shift from rationalism towards magical thinking, then this is not the first time the shift has happened. It would be more appropriate to study and understand magical thinking and how best to manage it – rather than deny it.

Taking a cue from the Economist's concerns: imagine that someone wants to persuade people to vote for Brexit. There are two main ways to do this: by rational argument or by magic. There were a lot of rational arguments, mostly against Brexit: along the lines that it is important to maintain Europe as a powerful trading bloc, about the time and effort of disentangling and so on.

But one can counter any number of rational arguments with a slogan – let's try "England for the English!" What makes this so different from a rational argument? It has, after all a certain elemental logic.

A key difference is that one cannot keep repeating an argument, because it begins to lose its power. A complex argument might need to be said several times before people fully understand it, but if you keep on repeating it after that point, then people's minds shut down – they don't want to hear the same thing repeated over and over again once they've got the idea. On the other hand a slogan is magic, it is an incantation: the more you repeat it, the more momentum it builds. If an orator was putting forward a rational argument for Brexit and the audience start to shout "England for the English! England for the English! England for the English!", then the slogan begins to dominate that argument. If the orator tries repeating the rational argument to regain attention, it is hard not to sound pathetic.

This raises a fundamental question: are such sloganeers clever black magicians, deliberately using occult powers to win an election? I do not believe as much. This is surely an example of the Sorcerer's Apprentice story. These mindbenders do not understand that they are raising a spirit, instead they believe that they are simply applying a formula. Maybe they studied the demographics of the English population to determine the level of nationalism and decided that a slogan like "England for the English" would attract a certain percentage of votes and so they adopt it as a formula they might use then put aside. They do not fully grasp that they are actually invoking a spirit.

So what is this spirit they are invoking? It is a rather lovely spirit: it embodies cottage gardens with rambling roses; it's about cricket on the village green and a pint of beer that is refreshing but not too cold; it's about a sense of fair play and so on. It is a lovely thing they are invoking, but a spirit is not a machine one can switch on and off, it is a living entity. Think of that beautiful spirit as more like a beautiful cat, than a clockwork toy. The cat is a lovely thing, but if you mistreat or neglect it, then it can scratch and turn into a hellcat. That spirit of Englishness includes being unusually tolerant of differences and eccentricities – an ability to welcome people who are different. But when that spirit starts to feel insecure, threatened or frightened it turns inward and against outsiders. Another English tendency is a sense of self-deprecating modesty: "No I'm not really a pianist, I've only been playing for 20 years." But the shadow of that nature is a level of arrogance that assumes the God-given right to colonize the rest of the world. Drive a lovely spirit into a bad mood and it can be bloody awful.

I suspect that this sort of abuse has marred the Brexit debate on both sides. People thought they could rely on slogans to work for them – just using a simple formula to win people over – and they probably didn't realise the extent to which they were actually invoking spirits. If they understood that better, they might not have caused so much harm. It's the story of The Sorcerer's

Apprentice: we learnt a bit of magic and called up the spirits to fetch water and they flooded the whole laboratory.

In my book I argue that moving forward from scientific thinking towards magical thinking is a fairly natural way to address growing complexity – just as happened around 2,000 years ago when we went from Platonic ideas on the supremacy of objective truth to the Aristotelian greater emphasis on observation. This transition is reflected in the Bible when Pontius Pilate, judging Jesus, asked "what is truth?" Was that really what he asked? You might expect a judge to ask "what is THE truth?" but not the post-modern version "what is truth?".

Going back to that Derren Brown and Dawkins interview, one thing was clear: they both felt that the post-modern academic questioning of the nature of truth was a serious threat. There is a suggestion here that a post truth world is necessarily one where there is no truth, that the masses are being lead to believe that "nothing is true", and so to distrust science. There is something inherently paradoxical in the claim that "nothing is true" – because it obviously implies that "nothing is true" cannot itself be true. (Incidentally, the actual value of the statement lies in its paradox. It could be used like a Zen koan to lead one to mystical illumination. But that possibility is hardly going to take the world by storm, as feared by rationalists.)

So a denial of truth bears little relation to the magical thinking that I describe in *My Years of Magical Thinking*. There is no claim that Plato got it wrong, that there are no absolutes such as objective truth. It simply suggests that we have got our priorities wrong: to be debating, arguing, fighting and even going to war over different beliefs about what is or is not ultimately true, when we would do better to focus on what we individually experience in the moment. We should be exploring and understanding the pond we actually live in before fighting over theories about the airy world that is assumed to lie above the pond.

It is a question of emphasis. The truth might be that your friend looks uncomfortable in his new suit, but if he's on his way to a job interview it is probably more appropriate to say: "You look great! You will win them over!" It is also a question of degree, of being sensitive to feeling: if he really does look ludicrous in that suit, more likely to fail his interview, then you might do better to admit as much.

We are not sliding into a world of un-truth, we are simply moving to a world that allows equal weight to subjective experience. A world where we are allowed to admit that a tarot reading or a magical ritual could be beneficial, even life-changing, and that experience could be every bit as valuable as other people's claims that the tarot is the work of the devil, or that there is no proof that the ritual actually caused objective reality to change. A world where it is no longer a sin to recognize when magic works.

Afterthought to Post truth Politics

Chapter One focused on a comparison between rational and magical thinking. In My Years of Magical Thinking I outline a larger context that includes religious thinking. Whereas a magical culture emphasises the individual, religious cultures are those that bind individuals into a group with a shared ideology or beliefs. This results in another form of "post truth" that is sometimes more troubling.

In My Years of Magical Thinking I looked at the suggestion that a scientific statement has no value unless it is capable of being disproved, and suggested a similar statement that a religious belief has no value unless it is capable of being dis-believed. No-one could found a religion on the belief that the sun rises every day, because that is so self-evidently true. But one could found a religion on a belief that the sun only rises because the priests spend all night in rituals designed to make it rise.

So beliefs that can unite individuals into a religion, tribe, nation, political party, academic discipline, fan club or other religious grouping are necessarily beliefs that are to some extent absurd – either by fact or logic. My examples included beliefs that: god was born in human form to a virgin; that kicking a leather ball into a net is supremely important; that workers could rule the world and remain workers; that Jews are conspiring successfully to rule the world; that one can understand a culture by observing it objectively, and so on.

In a religious culture it is the knowledge that we are surrounded by people who reject our beliefs that gives the religious group a sense of coherence and belonging. Repeating or reinforcing these beliefs gives a comforting feeling of kinship – so when the belief is attacked one feels personally attacked.

In Chapter One I have given the example of a "magical" approach, where a slogan was deliberately created to bring about a desired result (and I pointed out that proper magical practice requires an understanding of the nature of such invocation). But in a religious culture something similar can emerge without being deliberately created by an individual "magician".

In that previous example, the phrase "England for the English" could simply emerge as a casual comment among a group of strongly identified English Nationalists, and then catch on as a phrase that encapsulates a profound shared belief. As in my later (Chapter Four) thoughts on conspiracies, it is quite natural for others to look for a source for such political/religious beliefs – ie a magician or conspirator who shaped the beliefs to serve some end. But it is worth remembering that sometimes these binding beliefs can simply emerge as egregores (see Chapter Nine).

Such religious identification with a belief can have extraordinary results. It can totally over-rule logic, observation or fellow feelings. If a person identifies with a belief that a nation or culture that they hold dear is being threatened by immigrants, homosexuals, Jews, atheists or whatever, then any criticism of that belief, or demonstration that it is false, can be experienced as a personal attack upon one's identity. It will actually *reinforce* one's commitment to that belief.

This is seen very strongly in social media that encourage very quick emotional responses without requiring the burdensome toil of rational, factual or aesthetic validation. Someone posts a paper de-bunking one's favourite belief and that person is identified as an enemy threatening one's own identity. A furious reply is immediately posted, one intended to hurt, if not to kill. This defensiveness is so urgent that one does not pause to read and try to understand of embrace the other's argument, any more than one would pause to assess the character and motivation of the enemy soldier in your gunsights who is rushing toward you waving a hand grenade.

In Thundersqueak I suggested that the challenge of the Age of Aquarius would be to reconcile Society (represented by Aquarius) with the Individual (represented by the opposing sign Leo). Humans have evolved exceptionally strong feelings of group identity (religious culture) as well as individual identity (magical culture). In Chapter Five I suggest that these abilities might be every bit as important for the survival of our species as human intelligence is claimed to be.

Surviving in a post truth world

I had completed My Years of Magical Thinking, in which I suggest that centuries of religious thinking had given way to centuries of scientific thinking, and we're now moving towards what I called "magical thinking". I argued that this is simply the way thinking and attitudes naturally evolve – it's happened in the past, it's happening now and it will probably happen again in the future. But for some people this shift is very threatening.

Among the characteristics of magical thinking, as I described it, is a lesser emphasis on whether something is *true* than on whether it *works*, or is *effective*. For example, many people go to astrologers, tarot readers or diviners to find out advice on their lives – but what percentage of them go in order to get definitive proof but the Tarot works, that it is "true"? Surely the bulk of clients go because they want useful advice about their lives, or they want some inspiration or help. They are more interested in whether the Tarot gives them good readings than whether there is literal truth in the idea that the tarot encapsulates the wisdom of the ancient Egyptians, superhuman forces or whatever.

That shift of emphasis away from truth seems threatening to people brought up in a religious or scientific culture, where truth is fundamentally important.

Now I know that the religious and the scientific cultures have different criteria for judging truth. In religious culture it's more to do with authority: does this fit the word of the scriptures or the Pope or the priest or some other authoritative person – maybe even the authority of one's own intuitive sense? Whereas in scientific culture the truth is more about whether it is in accord with accepted scientific ideas and whether there is solid experimental evidence to back it up. So the criteria are different: but both those cultures agree that it is very important to avoid working with dubious, discredited or untrue material. So the idea that we're moving into an age when people are not so bothered about truth becomes somewhat threatening: there is a sense of slipping back into primitive ways – being gullible instead of asking hard questions.

Actually, in a magical culture, people do ask questions – they are just different sorts of questions. If someone makes a statement, then it is not so much whether that statement was true, but rather "why did they make it?": ie what was its purpose, its objective, what was the speaker trying to achieve?

Take, for example, a magical text like the *Emerald Tablet of Hermes Trismegistus*. The *Emerald Tablet* has this statement variously quoted as "as above, so below". So I look up and see the blue African sky, I look down and I see a tiled floor: so I know this is rubbish, it simply isn't true. So should we throw away the Emerald Tablet and try some other book? Not if you're approaching it as a magical text. Instead you ask yourself "why did they put that in?" and you start thinking hard about it. *Above/below* suggests a hierarchy: is this actually saying something about the human hierarchy? that prince or pauper are both basically the same within? That idea can launch a whole train of thought. Or is it about the higher mind versus the physical body? Can we learn about the one from studying the other? And so on.

Basically what is happening is something that I have elsewhere illustrated using that famous parable from the Bible: the very rich man who on his deathbed tells his family that he's left them a fortune in his vineyard. When he dies, the greedy family rush to the vineyard and turn over every square inch of soil. They don't find any buried treasure. They are furious. But, come autumn, their labour has meant that they get an absolutely bumper harvest of grapes. They do indeed get a fortune in the vineyard.

That's very much what that sort of magical writing is about. In my earliest writing I used the phrase "incoherent wisdom", and the rough idea was that, assuming that the universe is risen out of chaos, then any statement that is logical and rational contains limited information – because this statement follows from that statement or fact, and so on – whereas a random statement has got a lot more random uncertainties. It is packed with information, because you cannot predict or deduce from one statement to the next. Ok, that's taking it a bit far, but basically I mean that the more chaotic a statement, the more potential work you can put into it. The more you can learn from it by studying it and asking "why was that said?"

So, people from a magical culture do not feel that they're sliding back into primitive gullibility. Rather they feel they're on a path of self-improvement or growth.

What does this evolution mean in terms of today's society? I explained in my book that advertising and marketing are basically magical thinking, magical practice, so I take as my example an advertising slogan that was extant for most of my early years: "Guinness is good for you". Is it true or is it not true? We'll come back to that later. Instead we first ask: "why did they say that?

A lot of people living in inner cities have experienced Friday nights when the streets were rolling with beer-sodden drunkards puking in the gutters – not a happy association when trying to market beer. So the advertisers tackle that head on by launching a more wholesome image – hence "Guinness is good for you".

I also explained in my book how magic depends on things that *can be believed*, ie the statement has got to "feel right" – which is not at all the same as being true.

By the standards of most mass-produced foods, good beer is based on pretty wholesome ingredients – fresh water, malted barley, hops, without much processing or unnatural ingredients – so it isn't too big an imaginative leap to accept that this actually is a pretty wholesome drink. What's more, it does taste a bit bitter, a bit medicinal. So it is not too difficult to go along with the game that Guinness is good for me. (In truth, it actually was good for me: because in my youth I inherited some Guinness shares.)

The funny thing is that eventually the "truth police" moved in. I cannot remember the date when Guinness company were told that they were not permitted to make that claim unless they could prove, to scientifically accepted standards, that it truly is good for people. They couldn't, so the advertisers, being wicked post-truth magical thinkers, simply added and L and changed their slogan from "Guinness is good to you" to "Guinnless isn't good for you" a statement that lies comfortingly outside scientific provability. In fact in Britain, and maybe other countries, a little red L in a white square denotes a learner driver: so, by putting the L in the middle as a learner sign they managed to build a campaign on the added suggestion that anyone not drinking Guinness must be a beginner, lacking in experience.

The point is this: instead of worrying whether this is true or not, or even assuming it must be true because an authoritative source said it, if instead you ask "why" they are saying it, then you are entering a magical gaming situation. Is this a game, like tarot or astrology, you might go along with? Are you prepared to play it? If you quite like the taste of beer and you feel that Guinness does feel good for you, then you could feel good drinking it. It becomes practical magic.

But what about now, when people are getting really upset about politicians that tell blatant lies and seem to get away with it? What is happening here? How can an understanding of magical thinking help if, say, a politician says everything that is wrong in our country is because of immigrants: they are taking our jobs, the country is going to the dogs, and we need to get rid of them?

Where I live there are plenty of immigrants working hard and helping the economy to grow. They are interesting people with different ideas and are prepared to share them. So it's hard for me to get along with that sort of stuff – I'm being offered a game that I simply don't want to play.

But what if I lived in some downbeat "Rust Belt" city whose factories have closed down, where whole streets of shops are boarded up, where there's people out of work and rising crime, and the church down the road has been converted to a mosque. Then the same game being offered might feel more attractive.

Some might see the state of their town as evidence that the politician is right, as absolute proof that what he says is "true". I'm not claiming that: I'm just suggesting that this politician's game might work for this town. It might be worth a vote. If his game plan includes a tariff on foreign vehicles and investment for this region's automotive industry, then the town might benefit. But is he simply bringing a dinosaur back to life?

It depends. This sort of boost can build momentum: the region might become a centre of automotive excellence, attracting forward-looking companies to fund a research institute and make this the Silicon Valley of the transport industry. If that happens, the people who voted for the guy because they believed what he said was true, will now be totally convinced.

The trouble with truth as a sole defining quality is that it becomes binary: something must be either true or not true. So truth tends to split society into those who believe and those who don't believe. It becomes what I call a "religious" society where those who don't believe are identified as heretics to be cast out. They must be evil because they don't believe, so you don't bother arguing, you don't listen to what they're saying.

Those who voted for him simply because they recognised a bit of magic that might help their region are less locked in. Simply balancing one game plan against another, they are in a less polarized state, a more multi-dimensional space: they simply happen to live in a town that, thanks to this guy's policy, is becoming a really nice place to live in.

Frightened people naturally shift to the right, and scared or downtrodden people often opt for the apparent clarity and certainty of right-wing solutions. When people are prosperous and happy, they are more likely to shift to the left. So when local people, who once backed that inward-looking policy, start travelling abroad and widening their horizons they are more likely to experience a bigger picture in which, although his magic worked well for their town, it might not be working for the country as a whole, or the world.

Politicians do not like this: they want that "religious" level of support from people who are totally on their side – my country right or wrong whatever the facts for or against.

What I am suggesting is that we might waste less time campaigning against magical thinking while struggling to make accurate predictions about the potential economic benefits or drawbacks of any proposed political choice. Instead we might embrace magical thinking and simply try the proposed strategy: play the game and stay alert to judge whether it is a winner and at what point it ceases to deliver benefits. Then post-truth politics would not be as dangerous as people now fear.

Right now a lot of people are frightened because the media promotes "truth" as the key criterion for making decisions and so a lot of energy is being diverted into a fruitless quest to distil truth out of complexity. Take Brexit as an example: a vote was taken, a decision made and the argument grinds on and on as to whether Britain and the EU will come out better or worse for that decision. Why not instead look around, observe whether Britain is showing signs of becoming great again, whether the North/South divide is reducing, whether society is becoming more equal and whether anticipation of relative regulatory freedom has started to improve life or not. Then decide whether it is still a winning game, and vote accordingly.

I do not know the answer. I am not making a prediction. On the contrary, I am asking questions that increase uncertainty.

During a major cultural shift, it is a mistake to build predictions based on the assumptions of the previous culture. At the start of the Industrial Revolution I guess a lot of people made dire predictions based on the assumptions of feudal society. As the digital revolution gathered momentum there were dire predictions built on the principles embedded by the Industrial Revolution. Now we are being warned about the potential dangers of digital transformation and artificial intelligence – and it's too facile to jump to conclusions about a post truth magical world.

Magical thinking erodes that sense of objective truth, but it doesn't insist that there is no truth. So in that sense it is not "post truth". The most committed chaos magician do claim that "nothing is true, everything is permitted", but that is not typical of the broad magical fraternity. As in my opening example of a tarot divination, it will initially be judged for its usefulness in resolving the current situation. A useful reading might be "unless you take steps now to clarify your job situation, you could face financial ruin next year". Then it might be an interesting scientific experiment to refuse to take those steps just to see whether that financial ruin actually happens – but that would really miss the point of the tarot spread. The value of magical thinking is not whether it's true or not, what matters is how well it works.

I offer that as some consolation in case you are worried about the present situation that has been labelled "post truth" but which might better be described as "meta truth".

Instead of denying magical thinking, it would be better to understand it and do it properly.

Conspiracies and demons

The rise in "post truth politics" goes with a rise in conspiracy theories. While I am loath to spoil the fun, I do argue that it can be a distraction trying to identify people behind the conspiracy when the more serious threat might be discarnate

Conspiracy theories they can be great fun, but they can be worrying. People get hooked on trying to identify the evil masterminds behind the conspiracy, when in many cases there is not any individual or cabal pulling the strings so much as a systemic flaw.

Sure, there may be individuals making a fortune while society or the environment is being destroyed: in my anger I like to think of them as evil protagonists in a sort of James Bond drama, and that they will suffer a vicious defeat. But the less exciting truth is that those raking in the profit all too often convince themselves that they're doing the right thing – they really believe in what they're doing. Failing that, there are others who are so busy making money that they simply do not bother to consider the consequences of their actions. Much less exciting than a great Bond villain.

I don't think enough people understand the extent to which any organization – a big business, a profession, the military-industrial complex or whatever – can act like a discarnate, self-serving intelligence, even though it may largely consist of people who think they're doing the right thing. Such a system is actually serving itself. That means it learns to keep up the appearance of offering benefits, so that people respect it and think it's a good thing; but at the same time it is doing things that help it to survive and grow. Like a cancer, this growth is often at the expense of humanity, its host. So think again about conspiracy theories and think what might be behind them.

I've been thinking again about conspiracy theories and their pluses and minuses. I know a lot of politicians and media pundits are highly scornful of conspiracy theories – the phrase is meant to describe something laughably stupid. But I believe that such theorising also offers positive or instructive benefits.

An interesting example came up when I was running an Arcanorium course on how to transform our boring everyday reality and make it interesting and exciting. One of the things that came up was this idea: you are standing in a long checkout queue, fed up of waiting, when you decide to imagine that yesterday a tall, mysterious stranger approached you, called you by name, and said "you are a seeker". You were told that you were among the chosen ones being recruited into the secret Illuminati. No-one must never ask to join the Illuminati, they will approach you. In fact: on pain of death you must never mention the Illuminati to anyone; nobody must know who is a member of it or anything about it – it just doesn't exist. Remembering that conversation, you look and realize that there is a distinct possibility that members of the Illuminati might be observing you at this very minute. Of course they won't give anything away, they will act quite normal, so who might they be? It surely would not be that redneck guy in the t-shirt at the counter. But wait! He has very carefully placed three six-packs of beer on the counter – six-six-six, is that a message? No-one else seems to have noticed this, but of course they wouldn't, would they! Listening carefully, you hear him asking for a packet of Camel. Camel is Gimel – the thirteenth path on the Tree of Life! Oh my god! What's more, a sign catches your eye: the street opposite the entrance is 13th Street, an amazing coincidence! You must try to act normal and control your excitement, this is just too amazing…

At a stroke, your boring wait at the supermarket has become a wildly exciting adventure, a gateway to mystery. Conspiracy theories can do that, they can make life very interesting. But not everyone gets such positive value from a conspiracy theory. For others it will haunt them, become a source of worry and paranoia: they might lock their doors and take the phone off the hook and so on. What they're worried about is negative conspiracies.

Now this is interesting to me. I can think of what seem like very obvious conspiracies: take the example of Big Pharma. If you Google the term "iatrogenic illness" – in other words illnesses caused by medical treatment – the results are quite shocking: the extent to which drugs' side effects cause further sickness. Sickness caused by the very people who are trying to heal. Big Pharma are clearly part of this conspiracy: just see how they clamp down, or lobby governments to clamp down, on alternative traditional folk remedies that would be available at very low cost and must be relatively harmless because they have been widely used for centuries. It all looks very much like a big conspiracy, very negative and quite threatening.

I think there's a mistake here: to focus attention only on the people behind this conspiracy, those making a fortune while other people die. I think it's a huge mistake to focus only on the people, rather than the system as a discarnate intelligence. It surprises me that rationalists find it very hard to accept the idea of discarnate intelligence: the idea that there could be willful intelligence outside of a human brain.

If I use phrases like sense of purpose, will, or my "conscious intention", a logical positivist will insist that it is just a by-product of a very complex flow of information through my neural structure. The question I raised in my *Little Book of Demons* was that, if there is survival advantage for complex neuronal structures to evolve towards conscious intelligence, then why shouldn't all complex information structures tend to evolve towards intelligence for survival advantage?

In such terms, the medical profession plus Big Pharma is a hugely complex organism supporting a massive complex flow of information through its human members, so why shouldn't the medical profession, Big Pharma, or any big social institutions or groupings have evolved some form of survival intelligence?

If you look at it from that point of view, it doesn't have to be an evil human being behind this conspiracy it could actually be the spirit or demon of the medical profession. As we know from planetary and other spirits, they will display both good and bad aspects: in other words there is an Angel of Mercury and also a Demon of Mercury. It is pretty obvious that the angel of the medical profession is about the desire to heal humanity, to make people well and to communicate good things. But there is also a demon in there too.

I am not saying no doctor has ever been evil – one or two headline grabbing examples would make nonsense of such a claim – but I would reject the idea that the medical profession is made up of greedy people deliberately making people ill so they can make more money. And yet the system as a whole, the medical profession, would definitely increase its power if it could make more people ill, while keeping up the appearance of looking after their health.

To give an example of how this demon could evolve, consider the over-simple situation of three big pharmaceutical companies each working on a cure for arthritis. The first one spends a lot of money and years of research and comes up with a product that worked well under laboratory conditions, but it doesn't really work in the wider population. Very few people benefit, it's a flop. The second company finds a real cure: tablets you take for about a month and – no more arthritis – that's the end of it. The third company produces a drug that definitely eases the symptoms but, unfortunately for many people, it has side effects: migraines, stomach upsets or subjects' skin goes crinkly. So, which is those three companies is going to do best?

Our first one has a product that simply doesn't work. They won't do well. The second company, whose product actually eliminates arthritis, has a problem: their success is reducing their market, because every sufferer cured is one less customer. They've got a real problem. But the third company – as long as it also sells other medicines to cure migraines, skin diseases and stomach upsets – is onto a real winner. People keep taking their arthritis cure because it has positive effects, but they also need all those other medicines to cure the side effects. If you just think in terms of dumb Darwinian evolutionary terms – the survival of the fittest – then market evolution will favour the growth and influence of that third company. That is how the Big Pharma ecosystem will evolve.

So I argue that a lot of the evil you see in the medical profession is not because there is a wicked person pulling the strings to keep the population sick and dependent, but it is the system itself that is looking after its own interests. Obviously the medical profession cannot forget its healing role, as long as it does come up with cures it will be highly respected and influential and it will survive. In such terms it has a positive spirit, an angel which is making people healthy, but it also has a negative side.

Another example I have used is tobacco – when I give this example people think I'm trying to defend tobacco sales, but that is not the case. I just think it's very interesting that cigarette packets now carry negative health messages – smoking kills, you are damaging your health etc. Those negative messages are presented to people at vulnerable moments – often people reach for a cigarette when feeling stressed.

Now imagine you are in a hospital: what is the commonest sentiment you hear expressed? It is "you're doing really well". When someone looks they're on the last legs, nearly dying, the doctor and nurses will be heard saying "the rest is really doing you good – you're looking much better today!" Everyone goes around giving positive messages because they know the value in the placebo effect and the value of positive suggestion. Any doctor that made a habit of saying "oh my god you look awful! I don't think you've got long to go" or "you're killing yourself" would be frowned upon. And yet the medical profession has persuaded the government to enforce these negative messages on vulnerable people.

Once upon a time tobacco packets might show a healthy rugged outdoors man – the Marlboro Man – a really positive image of rude health. I remember the phrase "for your throat's sake smoke Craven A". There was a time when it was compulsory for boys at Eton College to smoke because it was considered a healthy defence against sickness. Far from encouraging these positive suggestions, they have now been banned.

Does this not suggest that the medical profession, in demonic manifestation, is manipulating the government to magnify the dangers of an addictive substance in order to deliver more lucrative cancer fodder to its hospitals? Again, this is not to say that there must be evil conspirators within the profession who are deliberately working out tactics to destroy public health. Nor does it deny that interesting possibility.

To summarise:
- If conspiracy theories add glamour to your existence, enjoy them.

- If they upset you and invoke paranoia, enquire of the theories themselves if and how they might be benefitting and growing on the strength of your exaggerated concern.
- If you enjoy analysis, search the problem for some systemic flaw that might encourage the group mind of an outwardly benevolent group or institution to flourish at the expense of humanity and act like a cancerous growth.
- If such a process suggests itself, then you can go on to explore whether the conspiracy also needs evil human vectors for its survival.
- Then decide whether the best solution would be to eliminate the evil conspirators, or to repair the underlying system, or both.
- Finally, should you enjoy such thinking, think again.

Conspiracies Part Two

This piece follows on from the previous video – Demons and Conspiracies. *What I now suggest is highly speculative – just some ideas to play with. It is based on something I wrote for David Evans when he was producing a book which was finally published as* The Enduring Problems With Prophecy *but originated as a collection of essays around the buzz about 2012 and the end of the Mayan Calendar*

I'm not particularly into aeonics. It's not that I don't find them interesting but it's just that – to take the Aeon of Horus announced by Aleister Crowley – I've always said that in 1904 no-one suddenly woke up and shouted that a New Aeon had just started. Instead it is only when you look back with hindsight and notice the various symptoms that suggest that the year 1904 marked a significant turning point. So, rather than waiting all agog for 2012 and the heavens to open, I suspect that we might have to wait another hundred years before we could look back to that year and confidently declare whether or not it marked some great spiritual turning point.

So I told David that I did quite know what to write about for his 2012 topic. All I could suggest was that I might explore some fundamental changes could be happening, or would be welcome to happen. And the following exploration is one of the changes I suggested in the article. It is based on my re-thinking of Crowley's three aeons.

First, let me remind you about my previous "conspiracy" video. In it I suggested that our worldwide human society is accompanied by another society, comprising what I called "discarnate intelligences" in the form of institutions, corporations, philosophies, religions etc. My nomenclature might grate, because we are not encouraged to think of these as living entities with a certain intelligence. But I suggested that actually it's really quite interesting to treat them not simply as abstractions but rather more as demons and angels engaged in a struggle for survival.

I gave the example of Big Pharma – the pharmaceutical industry – that one can choose to see as a sort of angel producing cures to help people; but one could also see as a demon offering cures with bad side effects that oblige patients to buy further remedies so that its members amass loads of money to the detriment of society. In such terms, the human ecosystem we call "society" can be seen as host to a multitude of cancerous growths that offer benefits to justify their expansion, while at the same time serving their own survival at the expense of their host. Perhaps the tapeworm is a better analogy: people have been known to swallow a tapeworm segment before visiting an unhygienic place, because the tape worm protects its host by absorbing dangerous organisms and bacteria.

I was supposed to write about some potential transformation, so I chose Crowley's three aeons model: describing how an Aeon of Isis is followed by an Aeon of Osiris and hence an aeon of Horus – as described in my YouTube talk on *Crowley's Three Aeons*.

I described the Aeon of Isis in terms of the infancy of humanity, when we were dominated by the struggle for survival, breeding and nourishment. Isis represents motherhood, and I compared that stage of our development with a toddler needs to be giving simple moral instructions – do this, do not do that – rather than more reasoned explanations. We see this in ancient religious texts such as the Old Testament with its 10 commandments.

This is followed by the Aeon of Osiris, typified by male gods like Odin, Prometheus and Jesus: gods who sacrificed themselves for the good of mankind. With it came a new morality, not so much "do what I say" as "think what a perfect being, like myself, would do, and try to live up to that".

I pointed out that this development is really quite extraordinary: the idea that that a mighty god could sacrifice itself for rotten old humanity! I suggested that this presents a real challenge to the Darwinian struggle for survival – not in the corny sense of evolutionists versus creationists, but in a much more profound form. It suggests that survival might not be the universe's ultimate criterion for existence or meaning.

Again, I am not invoking old arguments about the mysterious rise of altruism – usually countered by reference to the role of genes in furthering their survival by allowing members of a species to give their lives in order to foster the survival of their genetic components. No, this is something more fundamental, a real challenge to the whole importance of survival: in the Aeon of Osiris we find religions that forbid alpha males to breed, that insist on celibacy. In no way is that helping genes to survive. If survival is not actually the ultimate factor, then what is? Or could be?

The idea I wish to explore came to me 10 or more years ago when my wife was working for an institution called The Special Investigation Unit (SIU) which intended to investigate major white collar crimes – things like corruption, and big business doing crap stuff. The SIU had the power to demand the return of wrongly made money and to seize illegal assets. My role was a humble one: it was simply *to critique their organization's mission statement*.

(A brief pause while I search for a sick bucket. I suffer a slight aversion to business jargon)

I was asked to look at their proposed mission and there was not much to say. It was the usual stuff about aspiring to best practice, to become the centre of excellence for investigations and so on. I really could not fault it but – from my outsider's point of view – I saw one glaring omission: that there was no reference to the eventual demise of this organization.

You see, what struck me is that, if you ask what is the fundamental purpose or objective of the SIU, it was surely to root out corruption and banish it from society. In which case, it could never really claim to have succeeded until it made itself redundant. In other words: ultimately it should have removed all corruption, in which case you wouldn't need the SIU.

Now I know that is paradoxical but I'd like you to think of it like this. Imagine that you are a young police cadet who joined the police force with the highest intentions. You really believe in what you're doing and the value of it for society and the good it does for the safety of citizens. So, when you read in the Police Gazette that the government is giving the police force an extra 70 million pounds funding and recruiting hundreds more policemen and women, then it would be utterly understandable that you should feel pleased, proud to be in this growing organization. But, if the point of the police is to make society and good citizens feel safe from the threat of crime, then surely it would be better news to hear that declining levels of crime were allowing a reduction in police spending? A real indication of the success of policing!

Again, a young doctor hearing about the growing number of doctors and "now we can boast a doctor for every X thousand people, whereas ten years ago it was XX thousand" you might well feel cheered by the news. But, I argue, would it not be better to be told that th town's hospital is closing down half of its wards to make room for tennis courts and a recreation centre for the surgeons, doctors and nurses who have so much time on their hands now that the population had become so fit and healthy?

I am presenting a sound argument, but one that goes right against the grain. Instead it is in the nature of every institution to seek and foster its own growth. If you are part of a big company and feel you are doing well, it is so instinctive to want it to grow and grow. But actually that means that we are in culture of almost parasitical growth growth, growth, growth – with everything struggling to hold on to and expand its position.

I think one of the examples I gave was about how in London you get these trade guilds – like The Honourable Company of Leather Workers or what not. A lot of these old trades that once dominated London's economy are now almost extinct but, as far as I know, none of the old guilds wants to close itself down or move to a cottage in the country. Instead they seek new trades to expand into. I cannot remember the details but it might be that the leatherworkers decide that plastics is today's leather and their guild finds a whole new industry to expand into. Basically all these obsolescent trade guilds were surviving as hosts to new industries, rather than just admitting that they has done a good job and that now was the time to close down or shrink.

Clearly all these institutions, these discarnate intelligences, are acting very much in the spirit of the Aeon of Isis, they are all struggling to survive and survival is their key driver. So might it be time for this global society of discarnate intelligences to evolve, as human society started to a couple of millennia ago, into an Aeon of Osiris?

In other words might they begin to evolve in a similar fashion to human society? Let us salute the great contribution made by all these splendid institutions, let us recognize that they have a vital purpose but let us also bear in mind that the time may come for any organization when it has fulfilled its purpose, and then it should graciously sacrifice itself for the good of humanity.

I'm not saying that we don't need doctors, police or Coca Cola, but that we should hold in mind that the ideal society would be one that provides more for a sufficiency than a surplus: a medical profession only large enough to maintain good health rather than to cling to the reins of power, to keep surviving and growing unchecked.

That was what I suggested in that article, and it raises the question: are there any institutions that are actually doing this now? Moving into the Aeon of Osiris? I can't think of a single example.

Can you think of any national government that, having established itself, announces to its citizens that: "our philosophy has always been to foster individualism and, as a nation we have done good work so that our citizens are very well educated, strong individuals. Therefore, as a direct consequence of our proud national culture, we no longer feel the need to be a nation. We believe we can open our borders and allow all people go free. We have several excellent institutions still doing necessary work, and these will remain for now, but as a nation we now disband ourselves, and our world class athletes may compete in the Olympic Games as individual citizens of the world."

Is that not an intriguing idea? I like to imagine that many years or centuries later people will look back and say that 2012 was when it all began. Some hope?

As an addendum, I would like to suggest a possible connection, something that I have noted happening in several occult or magical orders.

One of the saddest things discoveries that an aspiring occultist makes when seeking to join the perfect order, is the inevitable pattern: the way they seem to flourish and then fade or split up. I know the IOT is not defunct, but there was a Golden Age when they were holding these glorious events in Austria at Lockenhaus – I was involved then and it was terrific. But a few years later people were telling me: "It just isn't quite the same now. It's like the old fire has gone. What is happening?"

I wrote back with a little story along the following lines. *Once upon the time there was a beautiful plant that sprung up and everyone gathered around it and marvelled at its beautiful flowers. They gathered their friends and all joined in marvelling at this glorious plant with beautiful flowers. Then some began to notice that the flower petals were fading slightly, it was no longer quite as brilliant as they thought. It began to wilt as if the old spirit had gone. It began to shrivel into an old, desiccated, dead thing. Everyone was so disappointed, and they began to turn away. What happened was that dead flower went totally dry and the husk burst, scattering tiny seeds so the people who walked away carried some of those seeds on their shoes. As a result some of those seeds sprung up all over the world and flowered anew.*

Something like this happens in so many occult organizations. There's a time when they flourish and furnish so much excitement, so much good feeling – like the hippie movement for example – and then people begin to say it is old hat, it is getting tired, then it's dying out. And yet sometimes the important thing is not that beautiful flower but the seeds it sheds towards a later generation.

So could this be an example of the sort of model I was proposing? An institution, or culture, religion, way of thinking, style or philosophy that flourishes and then appears to pass its sell-by date? Can such an entity prove gracious enough to do that: not try to struggle along and try to force people to follow its coffin, but rather permit itself to die gracefully and concentrate its essence into the seeds it leaves behind?

Will the future be human?

A friend asked me to comment on a talk at the World Economic Forum by Professor Yuval Noah Harare called Will the future be human[2]. *What I wanted to address is not so much what he actually says – which was very well explained – but the reaction of the presenter Gillian Tett who says "this is a terrifying view of the future".*

I'm not especially into this subject, but I've come across it in the media and have heard other people saying it is terrifying: the fear or threat of artificial intelligence, or even the threat of being visited by more intelligent beings from outer space.

The idea seems to be that high intelligence is a form of power: to have higher intelligence offers "power over". The broader argument is that this planet is now dominated by Homo Sapiens – and the word "sapiens" means knowing. So it is our intelligence that has given us domination of this planet. Therefore, if we create a far higher intelligence artificially, might that too come to dominate the planet, and so dominate us? Many people find that thought disturbing or "terrifying" as was claimed.

In the past I have argued that one of the best responses if you're feeling terrified (unless you enjoy feeling terrified as in a fairground ride) is to start asking questions. So I'm rather glad that Gillian said this so we can open up this discussion. Because all I'm going to do now is ask some questions around how terrifying it might really be.

The first thing I notice is that when the media discusses the threat of artificial intelligence the people they quote

---

[2] https://www.youtube.com/watch?v=npfShBTNp3Q

are invariably professors, authors or otherwise highly intelligent people who really know their subject. That very fact invokes a dual response in me. On the one hand it is clear that such people are chosen by the media for one obvious reason: if intelligent people are saying this, then they must know what they're talking about, so we have to listen. But a more rebellious side says: "people like that would say that, wouldn't they?"

You see: if one day the world heavyweight boxing champion were to pick me up by the scruff of the neck, clench his fist in front of my face and shout "might is right", I'd be inclined to agree with him. But when he put me down and I was at a safe distance I might revise my opinion to: "he would say that wouldn't he?"

You see there's something a bit self-serving about highly intelligent people promoting the idea that high intelligence is the ultimate key to dominance. At an individual level you can easily disprove the assertion. Ask who dominates our society today? Sure, Trump, Putin, May and their ilk are intelligent, but not blatantly the most intelligent people on the planet. Similarly, if you take the people who are exceptionally intelligent – like the people making these pronouncements – they are not dominating our planet. If anything, I'd say their influence is less than the influence of pop stars and reality TV celebrities. So at an individual level this simply isn't true.

But maybe the more important question is: is it true in a group sense? Going back to the idea of Homo Sapiens rising to dominate this planet, and "sapiens" meaning "the knowing one" maybe it does make sense, sort of. The idea is that there were all these other types of homos, different species of advanced hominids, and they were all wiped out leaving only Homo Sapiens, and it was the "sapiens" bit that did it.

That is quite an attractive idea that seems to be taken for granted – but is it really so obvious? More recently there has been evidence that there was quite a bit of crossbreeding between Sapiens, Neanderthals and other "homos", so it might simply be that Homo Sapiens were sexier and out-bred the others? Maybe we should really call ourselves Homo Sexual? After all, when rabbits introduced to Australia began to dominate the environment and drive out native species, they were not celebrated for their intellectual magnificence.

Instead of simply assuming that it was our intelligence, or "higher" mind that caused our dominance, you could make a very similar argument that our dominance flowed from the fact that we are the most religious species on the planet. I am using the word "religious" as I understand it, which is the ability of humans in a group to totally dedicate themselves to some abstract idea – whether a god, a way of life (eg communists or Buddhists), or an area of land and its occupants labelled as a "nation" – in other words "religious" to me means a manifestation of tribalism. Sapiens are indeed prepared to fight to the death for an abstract notion.

This is not unheard of in the animal kingdom – individual wolves will fight to the death to save the pack – and certainly it is true in the insect kingdom as bees will fight to the death. But it is one thing to fight to the death as part of a crowd with your kind all around you, whereas I don't think any animal would do the equivalent of a human being who chose to live for years in an enemy culture, mimicking its ways, and then one day put on an explosive vest in order to destroy some of the enemy and itself at the same time.

I think we are the most religious species on earth. No other species can become so dedicated to an abstract idea and be prepared to sacrifice everything to serve it. As that last example suggests, it gives us immense power over other species. And it might even be more important than our vaunted intelligence.

Now you can also argue that we're also the most artistic species on the planet. A piece of music, a book like *Das Kapital*, or a symbol can bring out such feelings in us that we will go to battle united behind a banner. You could argue that the last World War was really a battle between Marlene Dietrich singing *Lili Marlene* versus Vera Lynn singing *The White Cliffs of Dover*. The way that emotional bonding around a work of art can inspire us is another very powerful thing that might have led to world dominance.

If you know about my idea of the four human cultures, you might guess what's coming next: I would argue that we are not simply the most rational species on earth, we're also the most irrational. We see it in our humour. Weaverbirds build beautiful nests, but I've never seen them lauding a Dadaist nest or a Surrealist nest! There's a craziness about us humans and if I suggest that could be another quality that made us so dominant then I would not be totally out on a limb.

In the 1950s – a very rational decade – there was a whole genre of science fiction in which outrageously intelligent beings from outer space do invade our planet and do conquer us with their super technology, death ray guns, zappers and things like that. But, to make a good story out of it, the invaders ended up being defeated; and the closing dialogue tended to be along the lines: "they were the masters of the universe; they knew everything; they had every possible power… but they totally underestimated the sheer doggedness of the human spirit". Or: "they just didn't understand the power of the love of a man for a woman", or whatever. That suggested to me that, even at a time of high rationality, there was a still an undercurrent of feeling amongst the public that super intelligence – for all the power it can give – is not actually enough to be deliver total dominance.

What I'm doing here is not arguing against Harari's content, I am simply suggesting that there could be questions we should be asking before we allow ourselves to be terrified by what he says.

He talks about the power of data, and a government that might know so much about us that it could predict and manipulate our every move. But more than forty years ago in *Thundersqueak* I published *A note to future tyrants.* Here are some extracts:

GOOD day, Tyrant. You have just come to power, or so you believe. You have been handed a file labelled 'Potential Subversive Elements for Investigation and Elimination'; and in it you have found my writing, with a memo to the effect that its author could be a dangerous de-stabilizing element in an ordered society …
Scientists have told you that as long as you can collect enough information about the population you will be able to predict it utterly. Your file contains facts about my intelligence, my stability, my extraversion, my love life, my reading tastes, my political leanings…
I eagerly gave them all that information of my own free will. As you see from my files I have worked for the Civil Service and I have worked with computers: that experience was the only way I could learn a vital fact. The fact is that, whatever the scientists say about progress, whatever the ideal of a streamlined flow of memoranda in a super bureaucracy, in practice it is always the same: too much data buggers the system. They now have a new super computer with one thousand times the capacity of the old one. They are going to ask you to insist on knowing more about me: my chromosomes, my metabolism, my ECG brain waves, my sleeping habits etc. etc. etc. All this will be fed into the machine, Then, they assure you, you will know all about me and be able to predict my every

move. But can you see the mirage they are seeking? They believe that if they were given enough facts about me, or any other potentially dangerous person, then they could model that person inside a computer, and so gain absolute power. From earliest times the chief's sorcerers have been making models of his enemies with just that aim in mind… But surely there is a built-in paradoxical snag: if they succeed in creating a computer model of me, then they will have not one but two rebels on their hands!

How can their computer simulacrum of me be a total description of me unless it possesses its own consciousness, its own ability to understand the situation of its creation and its own ability to sabotage the system with deceitful responses to input stimuli? In effect, how could they ever rely on the monster they have created?.... The rebel can breed indiscriminately within their own memory banks… By this paradox their method is its own defeat.

Some people have pointed out that, although the tyrant might now have a new enemy, at least this one is imprisoned in his system. It is not a threat because it is contained. I think this is naïve: because, for example, when the apartheid government caught Mandela and imprisoned him on Robyn Island, his global influence increased. He was able to do more to topple the government from prison than he could in hiding.

More recently, one could argue that the tables are turning, because of machine learning. Whereas my tyrant was possibly restrained by his police's finite ability to track and process so much data, today's deep mining algorithms could work faster than any human intelligence to analyse and detect patterns of dissent in the population. If anything, that would support my paradox: because it increases the likelihood that the created intelligent model of me could be a "black box" – ie something beyond their comprehension and so beyond control. The more autonomous the AI, the more it might turn on its creator. I think that there's a real paradox here and I haven't really seen it addressed in these discussions about you the dangers of big business and government knowing too much about us.

Returning to my opening focus, which was not so much on the possibility of what might be done, as on whether we should be afraid: my own experience suggests that this is a bit of a storm in a teacup. I have been buying things online for 20 years and so commercial giants should by now have gleaned exceptional interest into my buying habits and be targeting me with surgical precision. But the adverts that bombard me online and in e-mails are absolute crap. If that's the best that big data can do I am underwhelmed. I haven't experienced any social media targeting that is half as good as an average human sales rep, and yet people are already expressing horror at the mighty powers of social media.

Going back to the more fundamental question of whether greater intelligence means greater dominance, I pointed out that there was little evidence of this among the human population. Looking at on a larger scale, I reckoned that it would not be enough for machines to merely outstrip us in intelligence, unless they could also outstrip our other non-rational features like religious fervour, herd behaviour and craziness. I think there are many questions like this that need to be asked.

The super intelligence most people worry about is an intelligence created by specialization, machines created specifically to be intelligent. But I do not see much evidence that specialization is the key to evolutionary dominance. In *My Years of Magical Thinking* I compare the popular idea of linear progress from magical towards scientific thinking with my suggestion that society actually tends to churn endlessly between magical, artistic, religious and scientific forms of thinking – and maybe that very diversity is what has kept humanity from specialising into an evolutionary niche.

The tiger's strength, the size of the dinosaur or whale – with specialist adaptation creatures have risen to dominate particular ecological niches and become endangered when those niches collapse. Whereas human's strength lies in relative non-specialisation and remaining flexible.

In fact humanity is increasingly having to expend resources on defending and maintaining species of animal and plant that are too specialized to survive the ecological side effects of human ubiquity and waste. If we develop machines that specialise in intelligence, might we simply be creating a new dependent species – too clever to survive? I see this happening already: I have used Apple computers for years because they could do useful things and increase my productivity. But in the last year or two they have become more delicate and needy, wanting endless software updates and to be constantly reminded of passwords they have forgotten.

Around 2000 I was introduced to Skype: a simple form of communication so brilliant that it almost totally replaced my telephone. But since being taken over by Microsoft it has been increasingly crippled: you have to go through tiresome procedures to issue new passwords every time, then dig down through useless gimmicks to see a list of online correspondents, and the quality can be appalling. Some days now I spend more time and effort nursing my computer systems back to life than actually getting any productive work done.

This surely is another possibility not often considered in these discussions: that humanity might become dominated not from above but below. We might be enslaved by the demands of nursing our latest pets: "super intelligences" so handicapped and needy that they demand our constant attention and counselling.

In response to Harare's question I might answer: "yes, the future could be human. All too human."

A crisis in democracy?

Something suggests to me that democracy worldwide is in crisis, and the reason is pretty obvious: society has given away its power and is divided. I suggest that the solution would be simple – if only we could live with simple answers.

In the nineties people loved talking about "empowerment" as though power was a great thing. I'm not so sure it is. Because the problem of power is that you only really enjoy power when you are giving it away.

I have a very powerful Danish LED torch: when fully charged it has a hugely powerful battery, but I only really *feel* the power when I switch it and it starts giving away its power as a beam of light.

A politician or dictator who declares war on an enemy must feel very powerful. But if you think about the day before he made that decision, he had almost twice as much power: because he still had the power either to declare war or to remain at peace. The moment he declares war, he has given away half his power, and is now committed.

I'm one of those pathetic people who only really feel powerful when I'm shopping. When one is shopping, sales staff bend to lick one's arse: "sir, these look superb on you, and I'm sure we could adjust the price a little if you buy both…" But, once you've made your purchase, they turn to someone else. You are no longer in power.

The power in democracy is the power to place your cross against one party or leader. When I got fed up with Britain's political parties I gave up voting – until I realised that that single cross is actually a vote for two things, not one. It is not just a vote for a party, it is also a vote for democracy itself. So it is always worth voting, – no matter what you actually vote for. That was what was so great about Screaming Lord Sutch's *Monster Raving Loony Party*: it offered a chance to vote for democracy, without having to honour the usual mob of political wankers.

But your greatest power is when you walk into the booth without knowing where you are going to put that cross. As soon as you mark your choice, you have given away your power to vote . In *Thundersqueak* I wrote *In Praise of Apathy* and *The Futility of Utility* and things like that. If I were to try to sum it up I would say that, "if The People are to take back Their Power, they must understand that *the dynamo of democracy is half-hearted support.*"

Please take what I'm going to say with a pinch of salt, because I'm not a political person and I'm living far away from the Northern hemisphere in South Africa – next stop Antarctica. But my intuition tells me that democracy around the world is in a state of crisis. Democracy should mean power to the people, but I sense is that people are divided, they are divided and ruled. If forced to encapsulate my solution to this problem in a single sentence it would be this: *there are not enough people in the world who have read* Thundersqueak.

But maybe I should instead invent an example. It's too late now to say anything useful about Brexit, as the vote has come and gone. For that very reason I will use it as an example.

Imagine someone surveying people's opinions before the referendum, and I will now advise you on a truly empowering response to the question. I will do so by presenting a parody of three common types of response.

1. Brexit? Oh indeed! Britain was once a great nation; it ruled the waves; it had a mighty Empire on which the Sun never set; and we powered the Industrial Revolution. So the very idea that Britain – whose democracy is an example to the world – should be dominated by unelected bureaucrats in Brussels, is absolutely ridiculous.

2. Brexit? A disaster! Things have changed: Britain was once a great and powerful nation, a world leader, but now if you look at the actual figures… [data data data] compared with Russia… [data data data] with America [data data data] for China [data data data] etc etc… we are now a very small player, a tiny cork tossed on great economic waves. It is only as part of a bigger power block, Europe, where we still have historic ties and recognition, that we could retain any influence or significance. A united Europe [with data data data] is right up there with the big players, and Britain has already put so much time and resources into joining the EU that to throw it all away would be ridiculous.

3. Brexit? You mean, like, pulling out of the European Union? Well, I quite like Europe, you know, and there's much better coffee in England since we've been a member. And we've had some great holidays on the continent. So, yeah it's pretty good. But I s'pose I might vote to pull out for a change. When our old family doctor died they got in this young Italian doctor and my mum doesn't trust him the same. He's a bit sort of a smart alec, you know. So, now we've learned how to make coffee, p'raps it's time for a change?

So which of these answers is the most powerful? The first has great emotional power, the second with all its economic data has great intellectual power. Compared with those, the third is really pathetic, a very weak response. But which is the most *empowering* response? By such a criterion, the third answer blows the other two right out of the water.

The first two answers are disempowering because they give away power, but make the speaker feel powerful as they surrender it. Those first two answers give away to a politician exactly what he or she needs to say in order to win your vote, ie to manipulate you. Either to pump up the chauvinism, or to pump up the statistics.

But that third response will have the politicians quaking in their boots. If the majority of British people are thinking like that, then the politicians will be forced to deliver a lot more than mere rhetoric. Although clearly about to vote "leave", that response also makes it very clear that, if anything goes wrong, the support will evaporate. If next year the cost of Marmite goes up, or it becomes more difficult to buy spares for VW cars, or something, then it will be blamed on Brexit. Faced with that sort of public opinion means that the future government will be forced to deliver actual results.

That represents true Power to the People.

In an earlier video, I think it was the one about Magic and Power, I pointed out an inverse relationship between power and strength. I argued that people often say they want power, when strength would be a far better aim. It relates to the traditional tale of the two old men whose feet were bruised and scarred by years of barefoot walking. One suggested that they might kill all the cows in the world to provide enough leather to cover every path and make for comfortable walking. The other suggested instead that they only needed enough leather to cover their own feet.

So, I will leave you with the gift of a slogan: *Half-hearted support is the dynamo of democracy.*

Anyone for Panarchy?

I'm getting further and further from my real subject of magical thinking but, while on the subject of democracy, I have often wondered why the idea of panarchy is not being seriously explored.

Recently I did a couple of videos about "post truth" society and polarisation in politics. In the discussions that followed it became clear that there's a lot of stuff going on that people feel very unhappy about.

Democracy – the idea that everyone has the freedom and right to vote – has long been fought for, and the struggle came to its head in the 20th century with its challenges both from Communism and Fascism. Democracy is now established in many countries, and yet I get a distinct impression that it is delivering results that many people do not like. A principle that the majority wanted, or thought was good, does not seem to be working the way people hoped.

There is plenty of political debate, but I'm surprised I haven't heard people talking much about panarchy.

In 1860 a Belgian called Paul Emile de Puydt suggested a new form of universal governance called Panarchy – a bit of a misnomer because "pan", meaning "all", suggests that everyone is a ruler, and so the opposite of anarchy, which means there is no ruler. So panarchy ought to be the opposite of anarchy, but it is not. In fact panarchy is not about any one form of rulership, it is more about empowering everyone to a greater extent. As de Puydt wrote:

The truth is that there is not enough of the right kind of freedom, the fundamental freedom to choose to be free or not to be free, according to one's preference....Thus I demand, for each and every member of human society, freedom of association according to inclination and of activity according to aptitude. In other words, the absolute right to choose the political surroundings in which to live, and to ask for nothing else.

Before I say more about panarchy itself, I'd like to point out two problems about democracy that it helps to address, and why I am surprised that more people are not talking about it. I would love to know what you will think about this.

The first problem is the unfairness of the voting system. I will take America as an example – and please pardon any ignorance from this far distant limey. As I understand it, there are basically just two parties, Democrat or Republican. So it was really hard on the Republicans when Obama and the Democrats came into power, because here was a government that those people had not voted for and, as soon as the Democrats won and took over, America became a Democrat nation – where all those Republicans' taxes were going towards supporting a government that they hadn't voted for. It was even harder for the Democrats when Trump brought the Republicans into power, because they now had a government that the Democrats hadn't voted for and, what's more, their taxes were going to support a Republican government and its policies – which included scrapping several things like Obamacare that the Democrats had fought hard to establish.

So there's a real unfairness for the losers in an election like that. To make it worse, it was not as though there was a huge swing in American opinion, like 90% of the people were demanding this change in government. In fact it was really a very small percentage shift, a tiny swing in opinion that tipped the balance from USA being a Democrat nation to a Republican one. A small vote swing changed the whole country to a different political allegiance. That really is unfair.

Now the second problem is that, as a result of the power of that tiny shift at the centre of the spectrum, everything depends on winning the people in the middle, those floating voters sitting on the fence. This means that there's a tendency for all the parties to slide towards the center in a desperate bid to appeal to as many people as possible – rather than offering any clear philosophies, values or strategies which voters might really identify with.

In Britain, for example, a proper Labour Party should really represent socialist government. But under Tony Blair it weakened and became really no different from Thatcher party principles. This desire to catch voters in the centre means that all the parties tend to slide into something barely distinguishable. They may make a few appealing promises to differentiate themselves, but everyone knows that when they come into power nothing much is going to change, so we end up voting for personalities rather than serious parties.

Panarchy, as I understand it, addresses those two problems because it gets rid of all elections. With panarchy there is no vote: you do not *vote* for a party, you *join* it. Having joined it, all the tax you pay will go to your party.

This is radical. For a start, joining a party and paying your tax to that party becomes a serious commitment. Ticking a box and saying "let's try this crowd this time" is something one could easily decide on the spur of the moment – a mere whim requiring very little consideration. If, on the other hand, you will be joining the party and committing to paying it a lot of tax, then it had better be something that you really believe in, something that you can put your faith in.

So, for example,if we go back to the British political parties: there should be a Conservative Party which it is properly conservative, in the sense that it intends more or less to maintain the status quo – it will of course also move with the times, but only in terms of what has already been shown to work. There should be a Socialist Party which really intends to give everyone equal opportunities. There should be a genuine Liberal Party where the emphasis is on providing everyone with a good education and good health, so that less money need be spent on resolving problems that arise from differences in ability and differences in entitlement. There should a true Communist Party, that really believes in not owning personal property – and so on. Basically, there should be a few, clearly differentiated parties, so that any citizen can recognize ideals that they really believe in, and ones they would be prepared to pay for.

What this also does is it shifts the focus away from the nation, towards the party. Any citizen of any country might choose to be a US-style Republican, or a UK-style Liberal, or a Chinese-style Communist or whatever, as long as their party of choice has representation in their area and is open to membership. De Puyt was a bit more precise in his suggestion:

In each community a new office is opened, a "Bureau of Political Membership". This office would send every responsible citizen a declaration form to fill in, just as for the income tax or dog registration: Question: What form of government would you desire? Quite freely you would answer, monarchy, or democracy, or any other... and once registered, unless you withdrew your declaration, respecting the legal forms and delays, you would thereby become either a royal subject or citizen of the republic. Thereafter you are in no way involved with anyone else's government—no more than a Prussian subject is with Belgian authorities.

At this stage I would expect people who have not heard of panarchy to be very sceptical – how could this possibly work in practice? The answer is that something like this is already happening and has done so for a long time – for this is how religious affiliation works.

If I am converted to Catholicism, in most countries I could pay a stipend towards the Catholic church and there would almost certainly be Catholic churches in any big city, there would be Catholic schools, monasteries and maybe a Catholic hospital. If I moved to another country, as a member of the Catholic community, I could use similar facilities in that country too. If I became a Quaker, I could send my children to a Quaker school, attend Quaker Meeting houses. What's more in many countries there are large companies run by Quaker families where, as a Quaker immigrant, I might find it easier to gain employment. If I convert to Islam I could become a member of the very supportive Muslim community in any country, and so on.

So, if these political parties were organised along similar lines, in whatever country you lived you would not be paying tax to that country, you would be paying tax to the party you had joined, and you would have access to whatever facilities your party offered.

For example, someone who had just joined a UK-style Liberal Party[3] would be laughed at by his neighbour who had just joined the US-style Republican Party, because he would start paying a much higher tax than his neighbor: but years later, when both had growing families, it would be the Liberal's turn to gloat, because his children would enjoy a free or heavily subsidised education, as well as excellent medical care while the

---

[3] I made the distinction "UK-Style" because the word "liberal" has been abused in other countries – as in "neo-liberal". Whereas I understand the essence of liberalism to be freedom – eg a society free from poverty, sickness, ignorance etc – neo liberals seem to advocate freedom not for humans so much as for institutions, such as 'the market'. This is equivalent to refusing cancer treatment, because cancer "has a right to be free".

Republican was having to spend a fortune for similar levels of teaching and health. Each gets what they chose to pay for.

I think that panarchy has the germ of an interesting idea. It would encourage political parties to be much more clearly differentiated, for no one would go to the trouble of joining a party that failed to make its principles, costs and deliverables very clear indeed. And each party could be sure of members who were more heavily committed and keen to see its principles put into practice. For, if they were not happy with the way the policies worked in the real world, they might consider other parties and make a commitment elsewhere.

There is, of course, one very big problem. It is all very well sending your children to a liberal school and take advantage of a good liberal hospital and and maybe living in a liberal housing estate or whatever is provided by the party, but who would manage the policing and justice in this world? What would happen if a member of the Fascist Party vandalized a Jewish shop premises. As a Fascist this might not be considered much of a crime but, if the Jewish shopkeeper was a member the Liberal Party, it would be considered a very serious hate crime. So who decides what the punishment would be?

Clearly, something else is needed. It might be equivalent to a world council of churches. Or maybe that, while most of your tax goes to fund your chosen party, a certain portion might be put aside for a national police and justice infrastructure. It is in the interests of any party to provide its members with conditions where they can prosper, become wealthy and be able to pay an appropriately generous income tax – so the national body might instead be funded by something like value-added tax, in order to provide and maintain basic infrastructure such as roads, railways, telecommunications and a police force.

One other thing about panarchy is that no-one is forced to join any party. If you decide that none of them suit you, you can become an outlaw. If you don't join any party, then you need survival skills to manage by yourself. You might have to home-school your children, or go begging to a politically affiliated school in case they have vacant student places that they would charge you for. Or else you might form a little local community – effectively launching a local mini-party of your own. You would be free to do that.

I think that panarchy is an interesting idea that might not at first appeal to everybody, but it does offer to empower the populace, and it does address two big problems that are currently messing up the democratic process. So it might be seen as a new way of presenting and re-evaluating democracy.

There might be an initial gold rush to found new parties, because they do offer a significant business opportunity – consider the wealth of the Catholic church. But I would expect this to settle down with mergers and acquisitions, because providing a supportive global infrastructure would be a major responsibility requiring massive resources and depending on millions of satisfied, and therefore committed, members. Ideally you would end up with maybe half a dozen big parties each with its clear and distinctive ideological and practical agenda. As with religion, you might have sub-parties – though I would be very sick if the Liberal Party embraced those bogus liberals who believe in allowing freedom for corporations to the detriment of its proper role in nurturing freedom for the people.

As suggested above, parties could make their policies as rigid or easy as their ideology suggests: so an Ultra-Conservative Party might disallow women to join except under their husband's name, while a Liberal Party might permit anyone to attend any Liberal school or medical clinic – provided only that it still had spare places for people prepared to pay a premium price.

So that is the question I am asking: has anyone heard of panarchy? Is anyone thinking along these lines? It is an idea that offers both solutions and problems. But doesn't any political solution offer just that?

Egregores

I had listened to a podcast where Mark Tavish was talking about his book Egregores the occult entities that watch every human destiny. *I found it so interesting that I sent off for a copy and had just finished reading it when I recorded this episode*

I haven't talked about egregores previously. One reason is that I have a natural reluctance to use jargon – from the simple fact that I spent so much my time having to write stuff for the IT industry, which is so heavy with jargon, that I got a natural revulsion against it. More specifically, I tend not to use it in when I'm talking about magic and the occult for a practical reason: the world of occult and magic is divided into many different schools, and some of them are quite antipathetic to each other.

For instance: when I wanted to write my *Little Book of Demons*, I knew that if I started immediately talking about fairies, angels, devas – that sort of thing – some people would flip it open and say "oh this is New Age stuff". Then they might either buy it because it's New Age stuff, and then be disappointed if wasn't sufficiently New Age, or else they might not buy it because they thought it was New Age stuff and therefore not of interest. Similarly, if I'd talked about Great Gods Outside the Circles of Time, then someone might say "this is Typhonian stuff isn't it?". If I talked about thought forms and astral planes they might assume it was theosophy.

So instead of doing any of those, what I did was begin by just talking about office equipment and the way it sometimes has an uncanny knack of breaking down just when you're most busy. I said that people instinctively ask: "how did it know we were on a deadline?" but they feel a bit embarrassed about it, as a silly thing to say. But I argued that it's not only very natural human psychology to ask that, but it's actually a good question to ask – and quite a useful way to approach the problem.

Having read Stavish's book, I realize that Egregore is not only useful terminology, it also applies to one or two of the things I've talked about in in recent videos. So I thought I would just introduce the idea now and then look at one or two of my ideas in the context of egregores to see how it works out.

It helps to have a diagram showing the surface of the earth. On it are people – us. Of course the earth surface is fixed – rigid apart from the odd earth quake or things like that – but the people are moving around all the time on that surface. I think there's a term like "zoosphere" for this sort of sphere of human activity[4].

SURFACE OF THE EARTH

People communicate, have ideas, talk and have thoughts – so we could suggest a sphere going beyond and use the term "noosphere" to name a sphere of

---

[4] Tried to find reference to it when editing this, but I failed. I was right about noosphere, though.

57

human awareness, activity and thoughts. In theosophical language you can say it's where "thought forms" hang out. Now clearly the earth's surface is rigid, the zoosphere is full of movement across that surface, but the noosphere is something much more flexible – see the picture. You could imagine during an eclipse of the moon a lot of people looking up at the sky and thinking about the moon and how this noosphere might stretch up towards the moon like a bubble of attention or awareness.

Here is one example of what can happen with this sort of public focus of attention. My generation was born mostly during the war, so we grew up with the after-effects of war. I can remember whole city centres demolished by bombs. Central Bristol was a huge bomb site. Food was rationed and we heard everyone talking about the horrors of war. So naturally my generation was relatively pacifist and anti-war by nature. When we reached teenagerhood many expressed that by rebelling against the military "short back and sides" look: they grew long hair and chose flowing clothes, tie-dye and beads etc. They began talking about peace and love and such great ideals.

You can imagine all that energy in the noosphere forming a bubble of peace, love, make love not war, and all that…

What I am describing the hippie concept. As it grew bigger and more visible it attracted more people to it. So you got this great big bubble of hippiedom stretching the noosphere – and this is what one might call an "egregore" as something built up or inflated by human endeavour and aspiration – see the second picture.

HIPPY

LOVE PEACE

GOOD VIBES

NOOSPHERE

SURFACE OF THE EARTH

This is not just an arbitrary concept, because it has real power. Even if each individual hippy who was against war went into the street and said "I don't like war", nobody would notice and nothing much would happen. But with all the pressure in this inflated egregore balloon, that energy could flow down and power a huge demonstration on the streets, thousands of people with anti-war placards. You could say in retrospect that these demonstrations didn't have much effect, but at the time governments were frightened by it, police and governments were scared. il was a powerful thing. So an egregore formed like that can be a powerful thing: both bringing people together and growing stronger until it becomes a battery of usable emotional energy.

That is the model of egregore that I grew up with, because in the 50s and 60s there wasn't a lot of alternative magical ideas around, and in Britain it was mostly the books of WE Butler, Dion Fortune and Gareth Knight. That was how they would describe an egregore: and in Tavish's book William Butler is quoted as saying:

From an inner point of view we may see it as a composite thought form charged with emotional energy. This energy is a vote from all those who are linked with a thought form. For those in the group who know something of the psychic mechanism involved, it can be directed upon any chosen target. Obviously such an energy could be used for good or evil purposes, the intention of those who manipulate the energy within the collective thought form determining the way it is directed.

Another writer that I read around that time was Mouni Sadhu who says:

Imagine that an intelligent and well disposed man was able to concentrate his thinking about a good idea, giving it a certain form. He may then find others who have same or similar ideas, and so a circle of men may come into being who are all thinking along the same lines but in a different form. It is as if every one of them is repeating the drawing of a plan, placing a pencil again and again on the same contours. The thing grows in strength, develops an astrasome, becomes an egregor or collective entity.

That was the idea of an egregore that I had at that time, but I very soon learnt that there is a different model. Looking at the area that goes beyond the noosphere – if that was the sphere of human thinking and imagining, what would lie beyond? It would be the "spirit world". So the other idea is that egregores can exist out there in the spirit world even when people are not aware of them.

There might, for example, be an egregore called the God of War in the spirit world and it could take many forms – Mars, Ares, Thor or whatever. So there's a war god out there and the idea is that sometimes these gods come down to communicate with humans and open up a channel to contact us. Then the same sort of thing as in the previous model happens: that people gather in the God's name and put their attention and energy into it so it becomes stronger and stronger – see next picture.

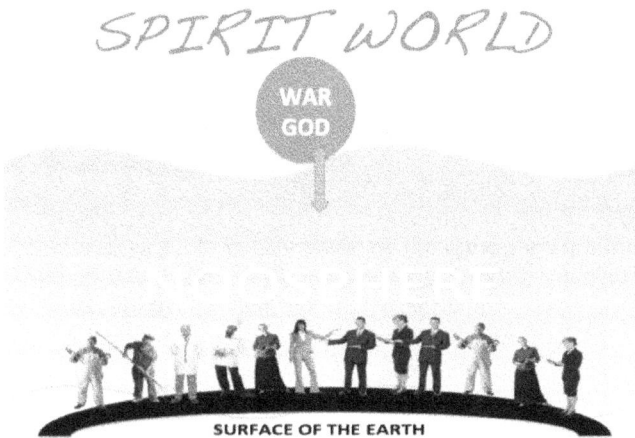

SPIRIT WORLD

WAR GOD

SURFACE OF THE EARTH

Given those two different models of an egregore, some people insist that they cannot go any further until they are sure which is the truth: either our thoughts are all inside ourselves, in which case the noosphere is just an abstract concept, it isn't real; or else actual forms can be built up and so the noosphere is full of thought forms; or is there a greater Spirit World beyond, where these egregores can dwell even if no-one is thinking about them.

Now I have always argued that one should not get stuck with such questions. People say to me things like: "when you were doing the Abramelin operation, were you trying to bring something out of yourself a sort of higher self? Or were you calling on something that is out there?" The point was I wasn't making that distinction.

If you are on a religious quest, it's very important to feel that you are on the True Path and not be led astray with a false path. Similarly in scientific work, although you may be less confident that there is a truth waiting to be found, you don't want to start working with a theory that's been discredited, so it is important to first ask which is the truth, which is real. But for magical work I've always argued that it's much more important to ask what works? what feels right to me? what works for me? And then to act accordingly. Otherwise, if you get stuck thinking "I cannot start until I've decided what the truth is" you will never get going. So that very interesting question about the true nature of reality is not one is going to occupy me at present.

In fact it is good idea to hold several of these ideas at the same time, because they often work well together. One obvious historical example for me was the Nazi Party. On the one hand there was the propaganda impulse: to deliberately build the egregore of the Nazi Party by devising a very powerful logo, the swastika in the white circle, and making sure it appeared everywhere on banners, posters, pamphlets, even china tea sets. Then gathering together literature, stories and movies about the great history of the Germanic people and how they had been cheated and crushed down and how they must rise up again. Then dressing the officers in smart, impressive looking uniforms and holding spectacular parades. All these activities helped build up an egregore of the Nazi Party and made it very powerful.

But I think there was another, more religious impulse: one that believed in this great spirit of the Germanic people that had been forgotten and ignored but was still waiting out there, and that these ancient gods were now calling to the downtrodden people of Germany to rise up and re-discover their greatness. The coming together of these two impulses, these two models of egregore, was an extremely powerful combination.

Going back to my idea of the hippie movement, it was definitely something new – there were no hippies before 1960 – but it wasn't the first peace movement of the world. There must have been peace movements ever since the birth of war. My parents met in the 1920s in an organization called the Kibbo Kift that advocated peace, free love and they believed in returning to nature for inspiration. Not necessarily that we should all live in nature – they were quite pro-industry – but that modern people needed to rediscover their roots in nature. So they would spend their weekends in teepees, doing strange rituals dressed up in green clothes and things like that. It was very much a proto-hippie thing that had been largely forgotten, but you could say that egregore was still out there, like a bubble. Then, in the way bubbles coalesce, it merged into the growing hippy movement. All that energy was already waiting out there. You see it works, it feels as though that energy is still out there, either in the noosphere or beyond.

If one night I spent an hour gazing at the moon and meditating on it and building a sort of "moon worship" egregore, the next morning in bright sunshine I would not need to spend a whole hour building it again: it's like I can close my eyes and be back in the mood. It feels as if the experience is out there waiting to be picked up again. Thus it makes sense (rather than reason) to use that model when you're dealing with egregores, rather than assuming that it must all be inside my head.

At the start of this video I explained why I have not yet used the term egregore in my previous videos, but I will now give some examples where the concept helps to explain what I have been trying to express.

I once spoke about Brexit and the difference between an argument and a slogan. You might have very good arguments for or against leaving the EU, but the problem with an argument is you can't just go on and on repeating it. Some arguments are complex, and need to be repeated in order to sink in. But once people have got an argument, if you keep repeating it too much their mind shuts off and they don't listen. A slogan is different: if someone comes up with something like "England for the English", that phrase actually gains strength if you repeat it. If a crowd starts chanting "England for the English!" it comes stronger and stronger like inflating an egregore. In the video I described it as an invocation: now I could say it would be like building up a egregore.

In the video I pointed out that there was a problem: people planning to do that in a manipulative manner probably think they are applying a "formula", meaning is a simple process that you can use to get a result then switch it off. I argued that this was a naïve idea, whereas actually they are invoking a spirit – what I could now describe as invoking and building an egregore. I suggested that it is a very lovely egregore: England for the English and you think of English country gardens, cricket matches on the village green, a great history of valiant archers and brilliant inventors. There is a whole world of very lovely things out there, and so the slogan seems rather appealing.

But I pointed out that such a slogan is not a formula that you can just switch off, an egregore is more like a living being: it's got a spirit out there, it's got a mind in the noosphere, and it's got a body in terms of the people subscribing to that egregore. As a living thing it's much more complex and wilful. Take any living thing, say a lovely, very friendly cat: if you treat it badly or neglect it, it can turn into a snarling spiky monster, it could be angry. Similarly, it's all very well sort of invoking this great spirit of Englishness if you keep it positive, but if attacked or treated with disrespect it can turn very nasty indeed. England can be incredibly arrogant and believe it has the right to rule the world; it can fight very viciously when cornered (like bombing Dresden in WW2), it can be terribly snobbish. There are plenty of negative characteristics which don't have to be manifest, but if you just let the thing go and don't manage it, then these negative characters can come out – because it's like a living being. Behave badly to it and it can hit back.

So people who think they are simply using a clever formula to win votes might find that they have got a real problem on their hands. That is an example of another thing that Mark Tavish refers to in his book – the negative side of egregores.

Going back to my bubble model: as you're pumping positive energy into the egregore it's blows up like a balloon holding more and more energy – all very positive. But human patience and persistence is finite, eventually people grow tired of pumping positive energy unless given a new impulse. How then can you keep building up the egregore?

Unfortunately, the best way of strengthening a tired egregore is to invent an enemy. When I referred to the Nazi egregore, one of its greatest strengths was that it was anti-communist – just as, for a lot of people, the attraction of communism was it was anti-fascist. The bubble can hold greater pressure or energy if you toughen its skin by focusing on its role as the barrier between outside and inside. We must strengthen the barrier against the enemy outside. This tends to change its character and bring out the worst in the egregore.

Think of the egregore's supporters as a cult with shared principles or beliefs. If someone decides to leave that cult, what often happens is that they are condemned, no one will speak to them, they are "sent to Newcastle". But there are many reasons to leave a cult: it could be because they're pissed off and no longer believe in the cult, but it might also be something quite practical – they simply have family commitments, an important career change or something that means they can no longer put all their energy into the cult. So this is very cruel behaviour towards someone who may have already put a lot of energy, friendship and commitment into the cult and made real sacrifices in its name.

Mark Tavish writes quite a bit about how one can detach oneself from such an egregore, to break out safely, because it can be a very difficult break. In a future talk I'd like to look at one or two cults and how they can hold people in and why it's so difficult to leave. It is a real wrench to pull yourself out when you've got a lot invested in an egregore.

When I spoke about my Abramelin experience I described an exercise I developed that I called "peeling off labels". It goes like this: how would the media describe me? Ramsey Dukes, a 73 year old English man, educated, six-foot-tall… etc etc. Now each of those is a label. I'm 74: okay, does that define me? A year ago I was 73; 40 years ago I was 34; but in a very real sense I am still the same person. So I can detach from that label, I can peel it off and yet remain the real me. I'm educated: okay, if I hadn't been educated would I not have been me? I would be different but, as a curious person I would probably have educated myself so, although that's a strong label, it isn't entirely me. So I take that one off and there's still a lot of me left. I'm English: but I've been living in South Africa now for nearly 20 years and could take on South African nationality – would I then stop being me? No!

I originally described this as "peeling off" labels, which isn't quite true, because in fact what I'm doing is rather "detaching from" labels: after all, I am still 74, I'm still English, I'm still educated so on. But I am less wedded or attached to those labels. The reason that this is a good thing is because each of those labels connects me to an egregore that enables others to more easily manipulate me.

For instance, I'm educated. So an orator or a writer who begins his speech by saying: "Of course, as every educated person knows… blah-blah-blah-blah… whereas the ignorant masses seemed to think that… bla bla bla bla" – that person is trying to get me on their side. As an "educated person" I might think: "yeah yeah he's right isn't he? Oh wow, so there are ignorant people out there stupid enough to believe the opposite…" and so I might be seduced into the speaker's agenda. But if I am less attached to that label, I am less inclined towards automatic identification with what he says. Instead I would listen more critically: "Is it really true that ignorant people think like that? I am not so sure."

It becomes much harder to win me over because I've detached from that "educated" egregore. Similarly, if one is totally identified with being British, one can be seduced by people who begin their speeches saying: "I'm sorry, but I'm not one of those people who's ashamed to call myself British!". If less attached to the British label, you might instead wonder why the guy is apologizing for something of which he apparently seems to be proud.

Consciously or not, it's actually a trick when he begins by saying "I'm sorry" for something he is actually proud of, because it suggests that "out there" is this huge majority mob that are desperately ashamed of being British, while he is one little lonely man making a stand against the mob. It is a call to arms for anyone else not ashamed be British. The truth is that most British people lie along a spectrum of ambivalence: they are proud of certain aspects of their nation (especially when hearing criticism from foreigners) but are also aware of aspects of Britishness that they feel ashamed about. The number of people absolutely ashamed to be British is negligible, and yet this orator is inflating them into a massive, threatening counter-egregore that needs us to unite and defend ourselves against it.

These are smaller examples than the big examples given by Mark Stavish where he talks about the pain of escaping from a cult, but I suggest that this exercise – of detaching from all the labels that society uses to define us – is actually a very good practice for not being trapped by egregores. Even the characteristics with which you identify strongly can be detached from once you really look inside yourself and ask "is that really me?" You realize that there is actually a lot more to you than any one social cliche.

In conclusion: what I want to explain in this video is that I have my own personal reasons for avoiding jargon terms such as "egregore" but, thanks to Stavish's book, I recognise that this is useful terminology. So I decided to look back on a couple of things I've talked about in past videos and re-phrase them in terms of egregores, to revisit them from that point of view.

Afterthought to Egregores

As an afterthought to Chapter One I drew attention to the extent that "religious" affiliation (in the sense of the root religio, binding together) is so innately human that an attack on an such an affiliation is felt as a personal threat. This also applies to the concept of egregores.

I want to emphasise the contrast between two strongly human characteristics: the "religious" tendency to sacrifice our individuality to a binding belief or group identity versus the sense that we have of ourselves as independent individuals. Confident individuals decry tribalism, the herd, cronyism, nepotism, mob behaviour. Meanwhile the voices of the herd – in the media, the pulpit or political speeches – decry individualism, narcissism, sociopathy or unsociability. But these two opposing tendencies are just derogatory labels for two vital principles. In Chapter Five I suggest that humanity owes its evolutionary advantage over other species as much to our extreme development of these contrasting principles as to our much vaunted rational intelligence.

Note the reaction to recent terrorist acts – from school shootouts to the terrible mosque attack in New Zealand. There is a powerful need for the community to identify the perpetrator as being a "loner" who did not mix or fit in with the community. There is an equally powerful need in the media to identify the perpetrator in the context of a terrorist "movement" – even something as broad as the "Alt Right" – rather than recognise individual choice.

In my afterthought to Chapter One I explained how a threat to a group identity closes the ranks against attack – so that counter facts or rational arguments not only fail to shift the defenders' position but can actually strengthen their resolve. This chapter on Egregores provides another language to describe this: it is the power of the Egregore to bind people to it and to transform the mildest dissenter into a dangerous enemy.

In another video, *I'm Gonna Blow Your Mind*, not included in this anthology I point out that in ancient times The Good, The Beautiful and The True were seen as strongly inter-related equals. But that the puritans in the protestant revolution demoted The Beautiful as worldly vanity, and the subsequent scientific revolution demoted The Good, leaving only Truth as our measure of value. Since then, digitization has reduced even Truth to a binary state – true or false – and this reduction has degraded all human experience and discussion.

In an interview on the *Weird Studies* podcast I gave the example of stem cell research using human embryos and how some people resisted the idea, despite sound scientific, medical and social benefits that could result. I suggested that the real reason for the resistance was not that they did not believe in the benefits, but because it was felt that using embryos was not Good. In this case, however, I backed the researchers.

Then I presented a thought experiment, shifting the context to Germany in 1940. Here the researcher might be using Jews captured by the Nazis for experiments to see how much the human body could endure in terms of heat, cold, radiation, poison and other threats. The research was justified for the enormous benefits that could result from the knowledge gained, and how it could save countless future human lives, at the cost of a few Jewish lives.

In this case, despite all the good potential, I would myself consider that the research was not Good. I would oppose it, and point out that each victim was also an individual human. Then the researcher explains that his work is actually an act of mercy. He is offering a quick death in hygienic laboratory conditions, instead of a lingering death from starvation, sickness, over work, over-crowding and torture that the Jews would suffer if they went on to the concentration camps. Now, the more facts he produces to back his argument, and the more photos he shows me of the conditions that he is saving his victims from, I might yet find that, instead of winning me over, I am feeling ever greater revulsion against what he is doing. My opposition to his research might go up rather than down – how obstinate!

Now compare this with what happened over Brexit. Both the leavers and the remainers threw up a lot of figures and rational arguments to support their cause. Some of those figures have since been exposed as bogus on both sides – life is not that easy to predict. Part of the strength of the leavers was that they added more emotional arguments to the mix.

But what interests me is that, now that it is clear that the economic arguments for leaving were mostly flawed, more Brexiteers are admitting that they were wrong and yet they insist that "leaving is still the right thing to do". This suggests that they are waking up to the fact that there are other criteria than the Truth of reason and facts, and that fundamentally they believed that leaving would be Good for Britain.

I am not suggesting that it would indeed be Good, but rather that it is worth opening up the tired old True v False tug-of-war to create a two dimensional playing field for debate: True/False in one dimension; Good/Bad in the other.

Let us put aside all the True False facts and figures for now and ask whether the Brexit vote has been Good for Britain, and I sense a lot of Bad: the country feels more bitter and divided than it used to be. So does that mean leaving is Bad for Britain?

It is not so simple. In 1975 Britain voted to remain, and after that came Thatcherism, Blairism and the almost total destruction of values that Britain held dear. So does that mean Remain is bad for Britain?

My point is not to provide answers but to suggest that we face a far more rich and complex future than is generally allowed for. One attitude that emerged briefly after the vote was along the lines: "the vote to leave is a disaster, but Britain has a way of only really pulling together in times of disaster." The Dunkirk Spirit. A suggestion that even an unpleasant Truth might ultimately trigger something Good.

Let us be totally pessimistic and accept all the arguments that Brexit is a disaster. Let us see a future where the pound slumps, Britain slips from being a second-rate world power to become a third-rate power, we become a laughing stock where we were once exemplars, our economy slumps and the population lives closer to third world survival levels.

Disasters on that level can happen to successful individuals. Read biographies and there are countless stories of people who hit rock bottom and later look back and describe it as a lesson, a turning point, the most important time in their career.

Those Brexiteers who once defended their position with dishonest arguments and fake data, but who now admit that they simply felt it was the right thing to do – might they actually turn out to be right?

That is at least a more interesting question.

Conspiracy Theories and the ANC

This was never recorded as a YouTube video. I wrote the original article ages ago, and it used my Big Pharma example then went on to compare that with the processes by which South Africa's ANC (African National Congress) was falling into decline. Rather than repeat that material I have edited the original to fit this collection. The irony here is that it is now generally recognised that the fall of the ANC was driven by a "real" conspiracy – and yet my thoughts about the way that this worthy institution's moral "immune system" became compromised may still have some relevance.

A conspiracy theory is a dangerous thing. For some, the theory becomes an excuse for hysteria, finger-pointing, witch hunts and reputational damage. For others, the very label "conspiracy theory" is reason enough to stop thinking any more about the problem. Few people can accept the idea of a conspiracy without conspirators: if none can be found, then it must just be a "conspiracy theory" that can, therefore, be ignored.

My Big Pharma example in Chapter Three – how the simple truth that "a patient cured is a customer lost" can foster a culture of iatrogenic sickness – may have been over-simple, but it does suggest ways that natural selection might drive the survival of dubious organisms at the expense of the host society. Scientific education has made it very hard for people nowadays to accept the possibility of such discarnate intelligence, and yet the legal profession does recognise that corporations can be responsible entities, and accountable for wrongdoing.

What suggested was that organisations and systems tend to evolve, through natural selection, patterns of "intelligence" that may serve their own survival even at the expense of their human hosts. Or – resorting to unfashionable language – that it is possible for a group of well-meaning people to become an entity that not only delivers real value, but also develops self-serving, demonic qualities. I also believe that, at the heart of such a growth, there is invariably some fundamental dilemma or paradox that should be addressed while, or even before, hunting for conspirators. In the pharmaceutical example, it was that "a patient cured is a customer lost".

When I first joined the ANC I was struck by the qualities of all the ANC stalwarts that I met – their intelligence, understanding and impeccable intentions. I had married into a family of struggle veterans and so was rubbing shoulders with many of the great names of the various apartheid resistance movements. Years later, most South Africans came to recognise that the ANC was indeed being destroyed by "Zuptoid" conspirators. However, I simply want to address the conundrum: how could this rot have taken hold while there were still so many conscientious and intelligent members in the organisation?

One fundamental aim of the ANC is to raise standards of education and prosperity among disadvantaged people, but the fundamental paradox here is that people whose standards of education and prosperity have been improved will become less likely to vote ANC. To some extent this is noted by politically motivated persons and, rather than analyse why this happens, they typically react angrily with dismissive phrases such as "middle class complacency", "clever blacks", "coconuts" or "capitalist corruption" – their own version of a conspiracy theory. The reality is far simpler than that: people who have learnt to read become more likely to discover other political parties and alternatives to the ANC; and busy, prospering people may be less motivated to vote than those whose only hope is in politicians' promises.

The equivalent thought experiment to that in Chapter Three is to imagine two contrasting regions in South Africa. In region A, the ANC governors are competent and dedicated: jobs are created, people become better educated, more prosperous and "middle class". In region B, however, the governors are corrupt and incompetent: schoolbooks are not delivered, medical facilities crumble, transport is non-existent and there are no job prospects – because the governors keep the government subsidies, save money by not delivering, and become extremely rich.

Then there is an election. While we might expect a small decline in ANC votes in region A, in region B the ANC vote actually increases. This is because people in region B know no alternatives, and the vote of such an impoverished majority can be bought by holding a party, handing out a few snacks and an ANC T-Shirt. In country districts it is only necessary to make promises to one leader to win a whole village of votes – "make sure your people vote ANC, and we will build you a mansion".

But how does this result look from the far distant perspective of the party headquarters? It appears that region A, with its decline in ANC votes, is failing to pull its weight; while region B is clearly governed by loyal and industrious party champions, who must therefore be rewarded by promotion to higher office. The worthy stalwarts who formed the core of the ANC now find themselves increasingly in the company of, and at the mercy of, incompetent, ignorant and/or greedy criminals.

A simple natural selection along such lines might explain why such a concentration of good intention could become diluted by incompetence, ignorance and sheer criminality. The country begins to suffer the consequences of severe mismanagement, the economy falters, the numbers of homeless and jobless rises and crime becomes the only way for many to survive.

When the party majority included intelligent moral activists, their presence formed an "immune system" that could defend against the worst excesses of corruption. But the tipping point arrives when the country is in such a state that the ruling party's best option is to re-position itself as a "liberation movement" that promises a new revolution – a curious promise from a government already in power. This happens when the leadership can no longer rely on the support of a shrinking minority of prosperous and contented citizens, instead it knows that its only hope now lies in an even less palatable truth: that the worse the suffering of the impoverished majority, the more likely they will be to vote for promises of liberation.

How could President Zuma be seen on television giggling like a school kid, to the cheers of his party faithful, at the very moment when it was being announced in parliament that over a hundred and thirty mental patients had died through government neglect? Why did the ANC under his presidency offer such enthusiastic support for every measure that encouraged economic collapse, unemployment, poor education and higher crime?

The answer is that, for a bogus liberation movement, every burnt-out school, starving family, business closure, rise in violent crime, abandoned farm or crumbling hospital becomes another opportunity to promise liberation and win votes. There is no better asset for an aspiring dictator than a burgeoning population of uneducated and unemployed young men: at the modest cost of a barracks, some food and a weapon for each, a bargain army can be created to terrorise the rest of the population and reduce dissent to zero.

At which point the presence of conspirators becomes very clear, even if it is still something of a mystery as to how the sickness could spread so fast and so completely.

In describing some of the underlying mechanisms that can allow a healthy organism to lose its resistance to corruption, I do not want to suggest that the processes are inevitable, but rather that they cannot be resisted without adopting a fresh perspective. The British National Health Service was for many years a success because it tackled its fundamental paradox – a patient healed is a customer lost – by adopting the Chinese model, where people pay for medicine while they are well, but not when they are ill.

Similarly, the ANC should ponder its wider remit. There is little value in promising education and prosperity for the masses while at the same time labelling those who have already benefited from education and prosperity as "enemies of the people". Instead it is necessary to give equal attention to building a society where the promised education and prosperity will be welcomed, enjoyed and shared by everyone.

Racism – it's Proudly South African

This was my satirical response to South Africa's obsession with racial stereotypes – as absurd as the English obsession with accents. I resurrected it when politicians, advised by a British PR company, made race their key message to voters.

I am amazed and puzzled by recent news stories of South Africans publicly denying being racist. Why are they not waving our national flag and embracing the label? What can there be truly great about our country, if not its proud tradition of racism?

Is this another example of "misperception", as highlighted by this year's Ipsos Perception Index[5]? The survey revealed that, from a sample of thirty eight countries across the world, South Africa ranked the absolute number one in our misperception of a range of data: such as rates of murder, suicide, teen pregnancy etc.

Consider my experience when I applied to become a permanent South African resident. I was required to meet a number of strict criteria – as is only proper for a great nation like ours. One was to indicate my racial type. Being somewhat proud of my dominantly Saxon paternal line combined with a Viking maternal line[6], I was pleased to tick the box marked "Mixed Race". But this was not accepted by the authorities.

I was told that I must tick the box marked "White European" – despite the fact that I was nowhere white: my teeth are mid ivory, my skin colour according to

---

[5] https://perils.ipsos.com
[6] I had my DNA tested and confirmed these wonderful histories.

Photoshop is around #bc9787 on the hex scale. Even the "whites of my eyes" is a misnomer (my hair had yet to turn white). But no, without even taking the trouble of sticking a pencil into my hair[7], the authorities had decided and ruled that I am now "white".

Later I visited the wonderful Cradle of Humanity museum near Pretoria. At the entrance there is a long colour scale spanning every shade of skin inviting visitors to identify their true skin colour by holding the underside of their forearm against this scale. There is no black or white anywhere on that scale. Such people simply do not exist in Africa, or anywhere.

Why was a supposedly revolutionary rainbow-national government making the acceptance of outdated colonial classification into a necessary condition for my being permitted to live in South Africa?

It was not that I objected in principle to this vague terminology. After all, our colonial ancestors had simply chosen a label to distinguish themselves from the strangers they encountered. Everyone did that as humanity started to travel across the globe. To native Americans, British were "paleface"; to Japanese we are "gaijin"; and the New Zealanders called themselves "maori" because it meant "normal" in their language. What offended me was that an erroneous distinction that had long outlived its usefulness was actually being made compulsory by the new South African government.

I could not comprehend the deep reverence that our ruling party still showed for the apartheid regime and its colonial roots. For years President Zuma subjected South Africa to his so-called "State of the Nation" addresses that dwelt at length on the state of the nation

---

[7] Apparently, this was a test used by the previous South African government to differentiate between races.

before 1994, but said little about the current state. Was he not aware that the government had changed? Why such rampant nostalgia for apartheid?

It is easy to forget that pre-1994 was a Golden Age for some, and not just the "white minority". Under the Nationalist Government our past president was a people's hero, a revolutionary, a liberation fighter. Now the great majority in South Africa merely see an old, greedy, criminal politician – living in a dream.

Following the advice of a British PR company, "black" and "white" became the very favourite words for his supporters – promoted at every opportunity in every public pronouncement. Little wonder that he chose for his favoured trading partners Russia and China – among the world's least "black" nations – and he only really warmed to the USA after it had replaced its "clever black" president with a proper blond-haired "white".

There was another condition that I had to meet when I applied to live in South Africa. I had to provide evidence that I had a big enough income, or sufficient capital to qualify for residency. Even being "white" is not enough, the government only welcomes "rich whites" to make sure there are enough around to take the blame for their own failures.

Should South Africans be proud of our world-ruling number one position in misperception? Should we aspire to greater realism by embracing such verities as our government's addiction to racism? Or should we encourage genetic engineers to create people who really are black or white – a shock treatment that might help the rest of us to appreciate being colourful?

Vengeful Gods in Today's Society

*I found this one after I'd sent the book for publication,
and throw it in now as it fits the general line of enquiry*

I sometimes wonder if people think of me as some sort
of expert, or a person of great wisdom? I see myself as
just an explorer – a person who asks questions rather
than providing definite answers.

In that spirit I wanted to share my immediate reactions
to a series of recent articles about new research into
what came first: omniscient gods or large societies. For
example: an article in Life Science[8] that points out that
*"when ancient societies hit a million people, vengeful
gods appeared"*.

To give this a context I'll go back to something I've
discussed in the past: the idea that our morality has
gone downhill. In Britain people would say: "In the
1950s nobody would steal from a neighbour, not like
now!" – as an example of how immoral people have
become. I pointed out that that may be true, but that in
the 1950s people believed more in effective policing:
that you wouldn't get away with stealing, thanks to good
old community policing. Now people are more inclined
to think that they can do it – so were we really so moral
in the 1950s? Or were people simply more afraid of
getting caught back then?

Going back further into the past: if past societies were
more moral, was it simply that they believed in God's
all-seeing eye and punishment? Is that real morality? If
the only reason you don't steal is because you are

---

[8] https://www.livescience.com/65039-punishing-gods-rise-with-complex-societies.html

afraid of God's punishment, then it's an open question. With that in mind let us look at what this article says. I'll quote some passages.

Past work suggested that the rise of this idea of cosmic enforcement of morality was associated with social complexity. The concept of supernatural judgment evolved to help strangers in large societies cooperate, researchers hypothesized. Some work, such as analyses of Austronesian religions or of the Viking age in Scandinavia, suggested that moralizing gods preceded complex societies, while other research, such as a study of Eurasian empires, found that moralizing gods followed the rise of complex societies.

But those studies were limited in geographic scope and hampered, at times, because historians lacked detailed information on the complexity of societies at given points in history, said Patrick Savage, an anthropologist at Keio University in Kanagawa, Japan. In the new study, Savage and his colleagues sought to overcome these limitations using the Seshat: Global History Databank, a database of information about global history from the end of the Paleolithic period up to the Industrial Revolution.

A lot of facts and figures are then presented. What was interesting is that they found the belief in moralizing gods – an all-seeing God who knows what you're doing and can punish you if you do wrong – usually *followed* increases in social complexity, generally emerging in civilizations with populations of more than about one million people.

"It was particularly striking how consistent it was [that] this phenomenon emerged at the million-person level," Savage said. "First, you get big societies, and these beliefs then come."

He then points out that in really small societies, like small groups of hunter-gatherers, everyone knows everyone else, and everyone's keeping an eye on everyone else to make sure they're behaving well. Perhaps like little local communities in 1950s Britain? Bigger societies are more anonymous, so you might not know whom to trust.

Now I'm recognise that from my limited experience with the Bushmen of South Africa. Hunter-gatherer groups, living close to subsistence, can't afford non-functional members, like idle lords sitting around. Everyone has to pull their weight. You might argue that the hunters, usually men, form an aristocracy while the gatherers are usually women: but when they hunt they are expected to share their spoils evenly throughout the group. It's just a natural thing because they know that on bad days they will depend on others success. So that is a good example of what he is talking about.

However, in communities of one million or more, you see the rise in beliefs in an all-powerful supernatural being, watching and keeping things under control. The researchers point out that they are not saying anything about the value of religion, whether it is good or bad, but only that there is a deep and consistent relationship with societies throughout world history.

For better or worse, religion is deeply entwined with what it means to be human. So there's that important distinction for me: the difference between a society where you do good because you are being watched, and a different level where you maintain your own inner scruples.

To give an example: let's imagine that you fall madly in love with your brother's wife, you lust after her but you know that this would be disgraceful, it could destroy your family if discovered. So you've got to watch your behaviour, knowing how close family members can be highly aware of each other – "we catch you casting surreptitious glances at her – is there something going on?" So you know you must watch your behaviour, make sure you don't interact too much, look casual. You might also make up for that forced restraint by enjoying the most amazing sexual fantasies about her when safely on your own. However, would you have done that in a religious society where God is always watching and where, in his eyes, thinking about sex is as wicked as actually doing it? You have to stop your mind. You might flagellate yourself, take cold showers, start praying: "please God Almighty keep me clean and honest". It's not just that you don't want the family to know, you don't even dare to think those evil thoughts if God is watching. That is very powerful, and I can see how that sort of belief could arise naturally for its power to hold a burgeoning society together and maintain stability.

Back to my example: where we no longer think our police are infallible, nor do we believe in an all-seeing God, does that mean we are more immoral or simply less scared?

I turn to another article in *The Economist*: a review of a book by Shoshana Zuboff called *The Age of Surveillance Capitalism*. I'll quote.

In this drama Google makes for a compelling evil genius. It started life as a force for good. In 1998 its founders, Larry Page and Sergey Brin, wrote a landmark paper explicitly warning that advertising-led search engines would be biased against the true needs of consumers. But their idealism was coshed by the dotcom crash of 2000-01, which forced them to turn a profit. Like Tarbell combing through Standard Oil's court documents, Ms Zuboff picks apart Google's patent applications to find evidence of its switch to surveillance as the means for its power grab. It was transformed from a "youthful Dr Jekyll into a ruthless, muscular Mr

Hyde, determined to hunt his prey anywhere, any time",
she writes.

It goes on:

It may be true, as Apple's Tim Cook has said, that "if the
service is 'free', you are not the customer but the
product". But arguably, only religions do a better job of
providing something for nothing. In a sign that people
value "free" stuff despite the surveillance costs, a
National Bureau of Economic Research paper has
calculated that users of search engines would need to
be paid over $1,000 a month to give up access to the
service.

So what are we looking at here? Imagine an artist
commissioned to paint a beautiful fresco or ceiling for a
church. He is inspired by Michelangelo's ceilings of
cherubic angels and all that, but also wants the painting
to look modern, the people to be definitely today's
people. It might make sense to do a Google search for
images for near naked children at play – dancing
around joyfully like little angels. But whoops! Aren't the
police looking out for people who do searches like that?
He might consider private searching via virtual private
network and such precautions, but this is a really hot
issue in our society right now. The intentions might be
honourable – just trying to get lovely images of naked or
near naked children playing – but what if someone gets
caught doing that?

With the level of surveillance being written about in this
article, and the pressure from the media and society,
the situation is every bit as dangerous as trying to hide
from close family that you're lusting after your brother's
wife. The more cautious the behaviour, the better the
concealment, the more it "proves he has something to
hide".

We are returning to the days when people really believed that the police are effective at hunting down wrong doers. He could get caught even though his intentions are pure – just trying to create an inspirational fresco for a church. We now hear stories about artificial intelligence analysing images and faces – isn't AI supposed to be even better than humans at judging people's sexual orientation? Might there be some subtle clues in the artist's FaceBook pictures or postings that subtly suggest that he is the sort of person who could come up with the unhealthy idea of searching for pictures of dancing children? As the sense of paranoia mounts, maybe he should not even allow himself to *think about* including any children in the picture?

Many people suggest that our society in this century is taking a sudden leap in complexity.
- As society grows more complex are we now conceiving an all-seeing, all-knowing God emerging to handle that complexity?
- Is Internet surveillance becoming the new vengeful deity, watching our every private move?
- Is that what society needs to ensure its stability through this chaotic era?

Those are the questions I am raising.